Love Divine

Love Divine

Lance Lambert

LANCE LAMBERT MINISTRIES

Richmond, Virginia, USA

ISBN: 978-1-68389-077-5

www.lancelambert.org

Contents

Preface

Lance Lambert shared five messages on Love Divine at the
Christian Family Conference held in Richmond Virginia in July,
1980. These messages have been transcribed into this book in
their entirety and edited only for clarity.

1.
The Divine Command

Deuteronomy 6:1–9

Now this is the commandment, the statutes, and the ordinances, which the Lord your God commanded to teach you, that ye might do them in the land whither ye go over to possess it; that thou mightest fear the Lord thy God, to keep all his statutes and his commandments, which I command thee, thou, and thy son, and thy son's son, all the days of thy life; that thy days may be prolonged. Hear therefore, O Israel, and observe to do it; that it may be well with thee, and that ye may increase mightily, as the Lord, the God of thy fathers, hath promised unto thee, in a land flowing with milk and honey.

Hear, O Israel: The Lord our God, the Lord is one: and thou shalt love the Lord thy God with all thy heart, and with all thy soul, and with all thy might. And these words, which I command thee this day, shall be upon thy heart; and thou shalt teach them diligently unto thy children, and shalt talk of them when thou sittest in thy house,

---

and when thou walkest by the way, and when thou liest down, and when thou risest up. And thou shalt bind them for a sign upon thy hand, and they shall be for frontlets between thine eyes. And thou shalt write them upon the door-posts of thy house, and upon thy gates.

Mark 12:28–34

And one of the scribes came, and heard them questioning together, and knowing that [Jesus] had answered them well, asked him, What commandment is the first of all? Jesus answered, The first is, Hear, O Israel; The Lord our God, the Lord is one: and thou shalt love the Lord thy God with all thy heart, and with all thy soul, and with all thy mind, and with all thy strength. The second is this, Thou shalt love thy neighbor as thyself. There is none other commandment greater than these. And the scribe said unto him, Of a truth, Teacher, thou hast well said that he is one; and there is none other but he: and to love him with all the heart, and with all the understanding, and with all the strength, and to love his neighbor as himself, is much more than all whole burnt-offerings and sacrifices. And when Jesus saw that he answered discreetly, he said unto him, Thou art not far from the kingdom of God. And no man after that durst ask him any question.

Shall we pray?

Our heavenly Father, we do thank Thee as we come to Thy word that Thou hast said through our Lord Jesus that the Spirit of truth will guide us into all the truth. He will take of the things of the Lord Jesus and make them real to us. Oh Father, we want to tell Thee, speaker and hearer together, that we are dependent upon that ministry of the Holy Spirit. We thank Thee for the provision Thou hast made for us, Lord. And we would together appropriate that provision, that this may not be a misspent time or in any single part futile. Let that Spirit of quietness come upon us all and grant we pray, Lord, that we may hear Thy voice and that the word of Christ shall dwell in us richly. We ask it, Lord, in His precious name. Amen.

God Is Love

I would like to dwell upon the divine command: "Thou shalt love the Lord thy God with all thy heart, with all thy soul, with all thy mind, and with all thy strength; and thou shalt love thy neighbor as thyself." The key to everything is found in the nature of God. One of the simplest and yet at the same time most profound statements in the whole Book is contained in 1 John 4:8 and again in verse 16: "God is love."

It does not say merely that God loves. That is a fact. Every one of us who has been born of God, who has tasted the salvation of God, knows that God loves and that He first loved us. But this statement is fathomless. It is profound. It is absolutely basic. It is all-inclusive. God does not merely love; God is love.

When the word of God says that God is love, it says far, far more than that He only loves. That would be wonderful enough; but that His nature is love is beyond our comprehension. We taste a little and it fills us with ecstasy. Which child of God has ever been touched by the love of God or filled with the love of

God to their measure and not known some kind of ecstasy, some kind of being carried out of one's self? I feel sorry for Christians who do not believe that there can be or should be any such experience. The more such experiences the better, especially if we are moving into days of suffering, and days of pressure, and days of strain. It is not that we want mere emotion or mere ecstasy or mere thrills, but we want to be touched with the love of God, and moved by the love of God, and filled with the love of God. To come to an individual and original experience that God *is* love is something surely basic. It must be something transforming. No wonder the early Methodists spoke about an experience that they called "perfect love."

God Is Light

"God is love." We must note that there are only two such statements and they are both found within this letter. The other is very like it. "God is light." You find that in 1 John 1:5: "God is light and in Him there is no darkness at all." Light and love are a theme that runs right through the whole Bible from Genesis to Revelation.

The co-relation of light to love and love to light is something you will find in every single book of the Bible. Take the words of the Lord Jesus which He put very simply in John 14:15: "If ye love me, ye will keep my commandments."

Again in verse 23: "Jesus answered and said unto him, If a man love me, he will keep my word: and my Father will love him, and we will come unto him, and make our abode with him."

Verse 21: "He that hath my commandments, and keepeth them, he it is that loveth me: and he that loveth me shall be loved of my Father, and I will love him, and will manifest myself unto him."

It seems in some Christian quarters that this matter of love is always put over against law, as if law is one thing and love is another, as if the commandments of God are one thing and the love of God is another, as if truth is one thing and grace is another. It is as if when you taste the love of God you are free from commandments, you are free from law, you are free from the word of God and its restrictions. It is not so! The Lord Jesus not only said it in these few instances as recorded, but again and again and again. So we find it in many of the letters. It is not that we have a whole list of regulations and laws to try and keep as under the old covenant, but rather that the Spirit of God has come within us with the law, and now the dynamic of the whole thing is love. Because we love God, we shall be found spontaneously keeping His word.

Some people say to me that they no longer have to keep the Ten Commandments. But that is nonsense! The Ten Commandments have come within you. If the Spirit of God has come within you, then the Ten Commandments, the ten words of God have come within you. You do not always think of *do's* and *don'ts*, but you just think of Him. And as you walk with Him you are spontaneously keeping the law of God. How can anyone love the Lord Jesus Christ and break His commandments? How can anyone love the Lord Jesus Christ and despise His commandments? It is impossible! If we love Him, we will be sensitively aware of every word that He has said. We shall be somehow conscious of the need to appreciate, to understand, to obey what He has said, not only in letter but above all in spirit.

Love and Light

Light and love—they are everywhere. Don't ever be sidetracked by some of the things that hold out some kind of experience of the love of God that frees you from the commandments of the Lord Jesus. We are in danger in some Charismatic circles of having such "bless me" little groups, the kind of thing where we all just get together to be blessed. We only think about ourselves, our own up-building, and so forth. It never enters our head that the Lord Jesus said, "Go, and make disciples of all nations." It never enters our head that He has appointed us to go and bear much fruit. It seems as if the only thing that worries us is just praising the Lord, worshiping the Lord, and getting our own needs sorted out.

We can go in the same way with the whole matter of the church. We can see church truth, but it can turn us inside out and upside down in the wrong way, so that in the end we become so church truth conscious that everything else goes by the board. There is no such thing as loving God without being aware of the full spectrum of His commandments.

It is not that we have to nail up the six hundred and eighteen laws that every good orthodox Jew must keep and somehow try to keep them rigidly. This would be a terrible bondage and heaviness to us all. But if the Spirit of God has come within us, then every single commandment in the Old Testament which has a spiritual meaning, if not a literal meaning still to be understood and held, must come within us. Isn't it so?

Jesus said, "Whosoever therefore shall break one of these least commandments, and shall teach men so, shall be called least in the kingdom of heaven" (Matthew 5:19). He said, "I came not to destroy the law but to fulfill the law" (see Matthew 5:17).

The Lord Jesus did not come to destroy the law nor to negate it nor to throw it out, but to fulfill it. Then, by His Spirit He came within us to keep it so that His law is written in our hearts and His Spirit is put within us. This opens a new gate, a new door, and it brings us into a new dimension of joy, of freedom, of glory. It is not a question of compulsion; it is not a question of duty; but it is the love of Christ which constrains us. For the first time our dynamic becomes the love of God because we were first loved by Him.

Love and Emotion

This love therefore is not what it is often understood as a kind of slushy thing, a kind of merely sentimental thing—we drool and are sort of doe-eyed. That kind of idea of love puts most men off right from the start. It is contrary to their nature. This is not the love God is looking for. Of course there must be sentiment in it, of course there must be emotion in it, of course there must be feeling in it, but this love is something strong and firm and rock-like. It is enduring.

This love is both the most wonderful thing about God and the most fearful thing about God. It is the most wonderful thing in the whole universe to be loved by God, but it is at the same time the most fearful thing in the whole universe. Some people think it is only wonderful. Let me tell you, it is fearful. Once the Lord loves a person, He will not let them go. He will relentlessly pursue them until finally He has cornered them, even if it is on their deathbed. In the end He gets from you what He wants from you. He brings you to the place that you ought to have come to, perhaps years before. Once God sets His love upon somebody, there is no escape. That is both our security and our fear.

Love and Discipline

Why does the writer to the Hebrews say, "Every son whom He receiveth He scourgeth"? It seems rather foreign to modern ears. But what it means is simply the security of a love which is firm, strong, and cannot be deceived or deluded. That is the kind of thing that gives a child in any family security. When they have the kind of love that lets them do anything, go anywhere, choose anything, be anything, they grow up insecure. But when there is a kind of love which cares enough to discipline them, cares enough to chasten them, it brings a security into that child's life. So it is with us. Oh, the love of God—how wonderful it is! How fearful it is!

Love Lies Behind God's Purpose

I want to say one other thing about the nature of God's love. It is what lies behind the creation of the universe. It is what lies behind the creation of man. It is what lies behind the redemption of man. It is what lies behind the goal of God, the end He had in mind when He created the universe and when He created man in His image. It is divine love that is behind all these things.

Sometimes in this fallen world when we see its contradictions, its depravity, its unhappiness, its anguish, its sufferings, the storms coming upon the righteous and the unjust, and the sun shining on the unjust as well as the just, we are tempted to question the love of God. But dear child of God, behind the creation of this universe, behind the creation of mankind, and behind that glorious work of redemption which was wrought by our Lord Jesus on the cross, is the love of God. Behind the goal of God, the aim of God, the strategy of God, the purpose of God, lies the love of God. From beginning to end it is a love story, a divine love story.

God's Repetition

Now I would like to take you back to the fifth book of the Old Testament, Deuteronomy. Deuteronomy means simply "the repetition of the law." Whenever God says something twice we need to give it serious attention. It is very interesting that each time God goes back over everything and says it all over again, it is with a very deep and great significance. All that we have in the book of Deuteronomy has already been given to us. The only new thing that is added is the death of Moses. Everything else is there. So why does God waste pages of the Book? There are all kinds of things we would have loved to have known. Are we going to eat in heaven? Are we going to recognize each other in heaven? What are we going to do in heaven? Is there a millennium or is there not a millennium? If only God had used all these chapters to pack in that kind of information instead of going all over what

He has already said anyway. We have Genesis, Exodus, Leviticus, and Numbers. Why go over it again?

God does exactly the same thing with the first and second books of Chronicles. Some of you probably have started on Chronicles and gotten lost in the genealogies. They seem to be endless, don't they? They go right back to Adam and then they trace the whole story from Genesis to Ruth through all those books. One might say, "Why waste all these chapters in the Book? Why not give us a bit more extra revelation, new revelation? Why go over everything again?" In particular it goes over the four books, I and II Samuel and I and II Kings. Why? There is a reason for it.

When you come to the New Testament, you have three gospels, all of which tell you the same story from a different angle. Then you have a fourth gospel, which was not written like the other gospels, but is an interpretation. It is as if that gospel sums up everything and says: This is the heart of the matter. With those others you have only part of the truth. You have the history, you have the facts, but you do not have the heart of the matter.

Chronicles does exactly the same. It is as if God put His finger on this matter of the house of God and Jerusalem and said, "This is the heart of the whole matter. This is the heart of all My persevering with mankind."

A Book of Love

The book of Deuteronomy is just like this. If you read the book of Deuteronomy very carefully and you have some knowledge of the other four books, you will come inescapably to one conclusion.

It is simply that it is a matter of love. It is an interesting fact that love for God or God's love for us is mentioned only once in those four books and that is in Exodus 20:6. But when you come to Deuteronomy, every chapter seems to talk about the love of God. It speaks about God loving us and choosing us because He loved us. This is why He chose you out of all the peoples on the face of the earth.

Then comes the cry: "You must love the Lord." Because God is love, only love will satisfy Him. Did you hear that? Some people are so used to it as a kind of gospel address that it just goes over them. Because God is love, only love will satisfy Him. Knowledge will never satisfy Him. Understanding will never satisfy Him. Zeal will never satisfy Him. Your work and energy will never satisfy Him. Your giving of your money will never satisfy Him. Even giving your body to be burned will not satisfy Him. Only when you love the Lord your God with all your heart and with all your soul and with all your mind and with all your strength will God finally be satisfied.

God loves you and He will not accept anything else as a substitute for love. But we believers are past masters at substituting work for love. We put work in place of love, as if by working our fingers to the bone, surely God will understand. If we give our energy, God will understand. If we attend meetings, God will surely look upon us favorably. But God cannot bear it. When the love is gone, it is obnoxious to God. Only love satisfies God.

You find this everywhere in the book of Deuteronomy:

"For thou art a holy people unto the Lord thy God: The
Lord thy God hath chosen thee to be a people for his own

possession, above all peoples that are upon the face of the earth. The Lord did not set his love upon you, nor choose you, because ye were more in number than any people; for ye were the fewest of all peoples; but because the Lord loveth you, and because He would keep the oath which he sware unto your fathers, hath the Lord brought you out with a mighty hand, and redeemed you out of the house of bondage, from the hand of Pharaoh king of Egypt." Deuteronomy 7:6–8

"Thou shalt love the Lord thy God with all thy heart, and with all thy soul, and with all thy might." Deuteronomy 6:5

"And now, Israel, what doth the Lord thy God require of thee, but to fear the Lord thy God, to walk in all His ways, and to love Him, and to serve the Lord thy God with all thy heart and with all thy soul, to keep the commandments of the Lord, and His statutes, which I command thee this day for thy good?" Deuteronomy 10:12–13

"Therefore thou shalt love the Lord thy God, and keep His charge, and His statutes, and His ordinances, and His commandments, alway." Deuteronomy 11:1

This matter of love is mentioned only once in those first four books and now as we go over this book we find it again and again.

"If there arise in the midst of thee a prophet, or a dreamer of dreams, and he give thee a sign or a wonder, and the sign or the wonder come to pass, whereof he spake unto

thee, saying, Let us go after other gods, which thou hast not known, and let us serve them; thou shalt not hearken unto the words of that prophet, or unto that dreamer of dreams: for the Lord your God proveth you, to know whether ye love the Lord your God with all your heart and with all your soul. Ye shall walk after the Lord your God, and fear him, and keep his commandments, and obey his voice, and ye shall serve Him, and cleave unto Him." Deuteronomy 13:1

"And the Lord thy God will circumcise thy heart, and the heart of thy seed, to love the Lord thy God with all thy heart, and with all thy soul, that thou mayest live ... In that I command thee this day to love the Lord thy God, to walk in His ways, and to keep His commandments and His statutes and His ordinances, that thou mayest live and multiply, and that the Lord thy God may bless thee in the land whither thou goest in to possess it...To love the Lord thy God, to obey His voice, and to cleave unto Him; for He is thy life, and the length of thy days; that thou mayest dwell in the land which the Lord sware unto thy fathers, to Abraham, to Isaac, and to Jacob, to give them." Deuteronomy 30:6, 16, 20

A Divine Love Story

I wonder if any of us have ever really understood the significance of Deuteronomy because what it is really saying is this: There is a divine love story behind your creation. There is a divine love story behind your formation. There is a divine love story behind your redemption. There is a divine love story behind your transformation. There is a divine love story behind your education and training. God has a plan for you and the Bible is the revelation of that plan. Some people believe that salvation is the plan of God, but salvation is only part of that plan since we are all fallen creatures. Salvation is the means by which God puts us back into His purpose, back into His plan.

The Bible is a love story. It begins with a marriage and it ends with a marriage. It begins with a marriage in the second chapter, and we are told later that this institution of marriage is a mystery. It is to represent and manifest the eternal desire of God for His own. When we come to the end of the Bible, we have a marriage. Only the marriage at the end of the Bible is between the bride and the Lord Jesus, the Lamb and the wife of the Lamb. Then wherever we look through the Book, it becomes clearer and clearer.

Most people look upon the little letter of Ephesians as the high water mark of revelation in the New Testament. In Ephesians we read these wonderful words: "Christ also loved the church, and gave himself up for it; that He might sanctify it, having cleansed it by the washing of water with the word, that he might present the church to Himself a glorious church, not having spot or wrinkle or any such thing; but that it should be holy and without blemish...This mystery is great: but I speak in regard of Christ and of the church" (Ephesians 5:25b–27, 32).

What an amazing book the Bible is when we begin to see it in these terms. It is not just the wrath of God or even the truth of God, but it is the light of God bringing us into the love of God and the love of God leading us into the light of God. Then the Bible becomes the most thrilling book in the whole world.

The Song of Songs

It is not for nothing that almost at the heart of the Bible there is a little tiny book that has been called by modern and liberal theologians (and I am not exaggerating) a bawdy love ditty. It is the Song of Songs. I prefer to believe the Jewish tradition concerning the Song of Songs, that it was a revelation given to Solomon while he was praying of the love between the Lord and Israel, His people. If that is so, it lifts that little book into the Holy of Holies. It is not just a question of salvation, it is not just a question of sanctification, it is not just a question of service, it is not just a question of work, or sacrifice. Suddenly we discover that God loves us with a consuming love.

There are three amazing little things in that Song of Solomon. When first she discovers that he loves her so much, she says, "My beloved is mine and I am his." That is where most of us begin. We have hymns that say, "Mine, mine, mine; I know Thou art mine." One old hymn says, "We will be crowned 'midst plaudits of angels of men.'" There is nothing wrong with it. Thank God, many of us will be crowned "midst the plaudits of angels of men." And He is ours, blessed be God. But that is where it begins: "My beloved is mine and I am his."

When we go on in the revelation of this amazing love story, we find that the bridegroom is not going to take it; he gets a little tired of her. It is not that he does not love her, but she begins to treat him in a kind of indifferent manner. When he knocks on the door, she sort of says, "I am in bed. I haven't got my shoes on, but I will come, dear." She takes an awful long time, slowly moving off the couch. But when she gets to the door, he is gone. Then she is seized with fear. There is a real love in her heart, but it has grown apathetically secure because she thought he was hers and now he has fled. She goes out and searches for him. She goes through the streets, saying to everyone, "Oh daughters of Jerusalem, where is my beloved? Do you know where he is?" And they beat her up. But she goes on looking for her beloved. Then comes the next great thing when she finds him and there is a change. She says, "I am my beloved's and he is mine."

A change has come, but it is not good enough for the bridegroom. There is a further experience she has to go through, and when finally they come to the marriage and the consummation of the marriage she says, "I am my beloved's." The "mine" is gone out. She has come to the place where she is his and she is secure in that. She doesn't have to say, "He is mine, he is mine, he is mine." It is enough to say, "I am his." And then she says, "What shall we do for my little sister? She is immature."

Strangely enough, it was not our beloved brother, Watchman Nee, but it was none other than that very respectable evangelical, Hudson Taylor, founder of the China Inland Mission, who wrote a book called Union and Communion on this very little book. He said, "Who can this little sister be? She is obviously related to the bride but she is immature."

The bride says to the bridegroom after they are married, "What shall we do about my little sister? She is immature; she has not come to the place where she can be married." And they say together, "We will do this, we will do that, and we will do the other until we bring her to the place of maturity."

And Hudson Taylor says, "Could it not be that those are the believers who do not go on with the Lord?"

Not every believer will be in the bride, although every one is potentially the bride. Who are those blessed ones who are invited to the marriage supper of the Lamb? They are not the angels; they are already there. It cannot be the bride because the marriage supper is in the bridegroom's honor. So who are the ones of whom it is said: "Blessed are those who are invited to the marriage supper of the Lamb"?

Oh, what mysteries there are of love in this whole matter! How you and I need to understand that the God who has saved us has not saved us in a mechanical way just to use us, just to manipulate us, just to fill us. He has not saved us just that we may be *objet d'art*, things sort of draped around the mansions of heaven like trophies that they used to have in those old manor houses in England—a hippopotamus head and an elephant and a leopard. Some Christians have the idea that since they have been saved and are now trophies of grace, God says, "Look at so and so. Ah yes, I got that one at such and such a time. And that one I got at such and such a time, and that one I got at such and such a time." No, no, no, there is something very different. The love of God for you is so consuming that it is like bridegroom's love for bride; it is like husband's love for wife. That is the story of the Bible, and that is why the Bible ends with a marriage feast.

In Revelation 19:6 it says, "Let us rejoice and be exceeding glad, and let us give the glory unto him: for the marriage of the Lamb is come, and his wife hath made herself ready." He calls her the wife of the Lamb.

That is why John said in Revelation 21:2, "I saw the holy city, new Jerusalem, coming down out of heaven from God, made ready as a bride adorned for her husband."

The First and Greatest Commandment

Now if that is the heart of the matter, listen to the summing up of the Lord Jesus. A scribe came to Him and said, "Master, Rabbi, which is the first and greatest commandment?" Now that question had always filled rabbinic minds. Only those who understand a little bit about rabbinical studies will know just how complex and analytical those studies can get. When I tell you that the greatest division that rent the synagogues in the middle ages was over how many angels could stand on a pin head, you will understand a little bit about it. That is not a joke; that is true. They argued and argued and argued as to how many angels could actually get on a pin head. Now that may mean very little to you, but there is some value in this analytical and complex approach to law. It has produced a nation of lawyers and scribes. That is why, when David Ben-Gurion, the first prime minister of Israel, was asked what it was like to be prime minister of Israel, he said, "It is like being prime minister of two and a half million prime ministers."

The scribe came to Jesus and said, "Which is the first and greatest commandment?" And Jesus replied in the age old way of the Jewish people by reciting what we call the "Shema": "Hear, O Israel; The Lord our God, the Lord is one: and thou shalt love the Lord thy God with all thy heart, and with all thy soul, and with all thy mind, and with all thy strength. The second is this: Thou shalt love thy neighbor as thyself" (Mark 12:29–31).

In the Matthew account, He said, "Upon these two hang the whole law and prophets." It was as if Jesus condensed the whole Bible into one commandment: "Thou shalt love." It was as if to love the Lord your God with all your heart, with all your soul, with all your mind, and with all your strength is to love your neighbor as yourself.

Consider the tremendous scope of His statement. He said, "The whole Bible is condensed in this. The whole Bible hangs on this. The whole Bible springs out of this." It was as if He was saying, "Do you want to keep the whole Bible from Genesis to Revelation? Then keep these two laws."

Note the simplicity of His statement. A child could understand this. "You shall love the Lord your God with all your heart, with all your soul, with all your mind, and with all your strength; and you shall love your neighbor as you love yourself." What simplicity! I wonder whether we believers have ever given adequate reflection and meditation to this basic statement of the Messiah.

Notice that He says, "You shall love the Lord your God." It is not that you shall love teachings or doctrines, although we are to have sound doctrines and pure doctrines. It is not that you shall love the concept of God. There are some Christians who love the concept of God. They don't love Him; they love the concept. It is not that you shall love the work or the service or the things, but you shall love the Lord your God.

Listen again: "Hear O Israel, the Lord our God, the Lord is one." It is not many things, not many purposes, not many lords; one Lord. Everything is focused on Him. What simplicity!

When a person is focused on the Lord their God, they cannot go wrong. When with all their heart, and with all their soul, and with all their mind, and with all their strength they love the Lord, the Spirit of God will keep them in the way, keep them in the will of God, and keep them within the work of God. You cannot do wrong.

No wonder Jesus said, "Because iniquity shall abound, the love of the many shall wax cold." If we are going to love things in place of the Lord, if we are going to center on organization or service or systems of things or teachings or concepts or truths instead of Him, we are in danger. The whole of church history has the evidence of this. People have gone astray because they have loved things or truths rather than Him. "Thou shalt love the Lord thy God with all thy strength."

Then I want you to notice the totality of His statement. When you think about it, it is hard, isn't it, because all of us, I above all, fall so far short in this matter. "Thou shalt love the Lord thy God with all thy heart, and with all thy soul, and with all thy mind, and with all thy strength."

"With all your heart." In Hebrew things, heart corresponds to spirit. It all begins with your heart; not with the emotion, not with the soul, but with the heart. That is where it must begin—with all your heart. If you love Him only with all your soul, you can go wrong, but if you love Him with all your heart you will be kept in the way.

"With all your soul." There are many believers who are frightened to death of the soul. It is certainly true there has to be a division between spirit and soul, but the human personality is the human personality. And the Lord Jesus gave this basic word to us all: "Thou shalt love the Lord thy God with all thy heart and with all thy soul." Don't be afraid of your emotions; don't be afraid of your sentiment; don't be afraid of your feelings.

"With all your mind." Some people cannot love the Lord with their mind. They say, "I can love God with my emotion but not my mind." Oh, yes you can. You can love the Lord with your mind. Your mind can come right under subjection to God and then your mind is released. There is nothing so petty or so small as great intelligence without God. I have heard the most incredible things said to me about the Book by very intelligent people, theologians.

I remember years ago being in a room full of men and being told about Elijah when he was on Mount Carmel and fire fell down out of heaven. He said, "Of course, we all know there is benzene on Mount Carmel. The trench that Elijah dug and filled with something that looked like water was not water. That is why when the fire came it licked it up. You have never seen fire lick up water, have you? But if it was benzene, of course it would." I was amazed by this explanation, and I remember in the question time asking him: "Where did the fire come from?" He was very surprised. Then I said, "Maybe it was Elijah's cigarette."

The point of the matter is this: here is great intelligence, which comes up with an explanation of a Biblical miracle, which is non-intelligent. The same man also said to the same people when questioned: "Well, Jesus never walked on the water. As we all know there are parts of the lake of Galilee which are very shallow. He walked on the seabed." But this was an even greater miracle because as I asked him later: "How did Peter sink?"

Quite honestly it is best to leave the Biblical stories as the Biblical stories to be accepted as they are written—through faith. Once you try to explain them and explain them away, what happens? You end up with intelligent people giving a very non-intelligent explanation. This happens when the mind is supreme, when the mind dominates, when our brain is the thing and even determines everything about God. No, we must love the Lord our God not only with all our heart and with all our soul, but with all our mind. For then God can give us revelation; God can give us illumination which is a wisdom far beyond what this world has access to and which is in itself totally intelligent.

"And with all your strength." In this summing up by the Lord Jesus of this whole matter, we find this divine command. Note that it is a command. God never commands us to do anything that through faith and grace we cannot do. If God says go and make disciples of all nations, we can do it by His grace and through the obedience of faith. If God says that we are to go and possess something, then we can possess it through grace, by His power, through the obedience of faith. So it is here in this matter: "Thou shalt love the Lord thy God with all thy heart, and with all thy soul, and with all thy mind, and with all thy strength."

Beloved people of God, we are entering into years of shaking, of change, of strain, of darkness, of strife, such as the world has not seen. Only the love of God will keep us. And that love of God will not be satisfied with anything less than or other than our loving Him with all our heart and all our soul and all our mind and all our strength.

The Second Great Commandment

Jesus said, "And the second is like unto it; thou shalt love thy neighbor as thyself." Some people feel, "I can love the Lord with all my heart, but to love my neighbor as myself—?" It is interesting that the Lord, in His wonderful, gracious way, did not say: "Thou shalt love thy neighbor with all thy heart, with all thy soul, with all thy mind, and with all thy strength." He said one marvelously simple thing: "Thou shalt love thy neighbor as thyself."

Some Christians, I am quite sure, feel it is quite wrong to love themselves, but God takes it for granted. Every one loves himself. The deepest instinct in us is self-preservation because we love ourselves. Sometimes it is inverted by people who suffer from a terrible inferiority complex. It is only because they love themselves even more than normal and they feel that somehow or other they should be more.

If only you would love your neighbor as you love yourself. If only you would care for your neighbor as you care for yourself. If only you would think about your neighbor as you think about yourself. If only you would think about the welfare of your neighbor as you think about your own welfare. If only you would think about the satisfaction of your neighbor as you think about your satisfaction. What a world it would be! Don't you think that we believers have fallen very, very far short in this matter of loving our neighbors as ourselves? We sometimes look upon our neighbors as sort of heads to be counted. We don't think of them often as human beings that God loves and Jesus died for.

Sometimes we almost think of them as kind of fodder that can be brought into the church. God does not look at it like that. Thou shalt love, not the multitude, but thy neighbor as thyself.

If we are to love our neighbor as ourselves, what about our brother and sister? There is so much in the Book about this. In Galatians 5:13–15: "For ye, brethren, were called for freedom; only use not your freedom for an occasion to the flesh, but through love be servants one to another. For the whole law is fulfilled in one word, even in this: Thou shalt love thy neighbor as thyself. But if ye bite and devour one another, take heed that ye be not consumed one of another."

This is what happens, doesn't it? Again and again, in the fellowships of God's people they bite and they devour one another, and in the end they themselves are consumed. The whole thing is swallowed up in backbiting and gossip and factions. Through love be servants to one another. It is not, "through love be masters one of another," nor "through love be teachers one of another," nor "through love be correctors one of another," nor "through love be leaders one of another." But it is through love be servants of one another.

In Galatians 6:2 it says, "Bear ye one another's burdens, and so fulfill the law of Christ." The apostle was quite clear about this statement of the Lord Jesus. He called it the law of the Messiah. "Thou shalt love thy neighbor as thyself." And it is interesting that the apostle takes the second part and says it is the whole law being fulfilled. It is as if he takes it for granted that you are to love the Lord your God with all your heart and with all your soul and with all your mind and with all your strength, and that the outcome and consequence of that will be seen in your loving your neighbor as yourself.

Who Is My Neighbor?

Many will ask the question that a scribe asked Jesus: "Who, Lord, is my neighbor?" And Jesus told a story. He said, "There was a certain man who went on a journey down to Jericho through the wilderness." Now the journey down to Jericho from Jerusalem is a four-thousand-foot descent through wild and wilderness country, and in those days it was filled with brigands and robbers. On his way down, this man was robbed and left half dead by the way. And there a priest came by, evidently on his way up to Jerusalem. He knew the law of God; he kept the covenant of God; he was a teacher of the word of God; and he saw the man half dead. Maybe he remembered the law that if he touched a dead body he would be unclean, so he passed by on the other side.

Then there came a Levite, one who was supposed to look after the things of God, care for the work of God, a guardian of the worship of God. He saw the man half dead, and he passed by on the other side.

I wonder how many fellowships here are passing by on the other side? I wonder how many groups here see people half dead in their communities and pass by on the other side? We are priests of God; we are God's Levites. We don't want to get involved with the half dead. We don't want to get involved with those who are mangled, half murdered, with their problems and difficulties. It will be a whirlpool. We feel it will suck us into it and take us away from the real objective of God. So we pass by on the other side.

Then there came a Samaritan and when he saw him, he had compassion on him. He dismounted, poured in wine and oil, bandaged him up, and set him on his own animal. As far as we know, he turned around and went back to the inn and said to the innkeeper (there was only one inn between Jerusalem and Jericho in the old days): "Keep him at my expense until I come again." And Jesus said, "Who was the good neighbor?"

Sometimes it is better to be a Samaritan in love with God than a priest who is lukewarm. Sometimes it is better to be a Samaritan, mixed up, than a Levite who is separate from the world. If the love of God is not in our heart and love for our neighbor as for ourselves is not being fulfilled, it is our condemnation.

What should our response be? Jesus said, "Hear O Israel, the Lord our God, the Lord is one. Thou shalt love the Lord thy God with all thy heart, with all thy soul, with all thy mind, and with all thy strength, and thou shalt love thy neighbor as thyself." What will be our response? Don't we all come short, both as companies of God's people and as individual believers? Don't we all fall short in this matter? Is it not time for us to take heed lest we move into these days with a delusion, that we are right with God, that we are safe and secure, when perhaps our love has grown cold?

I think we can only take the word of the bridegroom in the Song of Solomon 8:6: "Set me as a seal upon thy heart, as a seal upon thine arm: for love is strong as death; jealousy is cruel as Sheol. The flashes thereof are flashes of fire, a very flame of the Lord, many waters cannot quench love, neither can floods drown it. If a man would give all the substance of his house for love, he would be utterly condemned."

May God really speak to each one of us, and may this divine command be fulfilled, be heeded. May we obey Him, cleave to Him, serve Him, and above all, love Him with all our heart.

Shall we pray?

Lord, we pray together that Thou will take these poor words of mine and make them by Thy Spirit like a sword in our heart, dividing between soul and spirit, discerning the very thoughts and intents of our hearts, the very motivating forces of our lives. Oh Lord, since Thou hast said that the whole Book is summed up in these two simple but profound commandments, find us out and give us grace that we may keep them and fulfill them. And we ask it in the name of our Lord Jesus. Amen.

2.
The Divine Challenge

John 21:1–25

After these things Jesus manifested himself again to the disciples at the sea of Tiberias; and he manifested himself on this wise. There were together Simon Peter, and Thomas called Didymus, and Nathanael of Cana in Galilee, and the sons of Zebedee, and two other of his disciples. Simon Peter saith unto them, I go a fishing. They say unto him, We also come with thee. They went forth, and entered into the boat; and that night they took nothing. But when day was now breaking, Jesus stood on the beach: yet the disciples knew not that it was Jesus. Jesus therefore saith unto them, Children, have ye aught to eat? They answered him, No. And he said unto them, Cast the net on the right side of the boat, and ye shall find. They cast therefore, and now they were not able to draw it for the multitude of fishes. That disciple therefore whom Jesus loved saith unto Peter, It is the Lord. So when Simon Peter heard that it was the Lord, he girt his coat about him (for he was naked), and cast himself into the sea. But the other disciples came in the little boat (for they were not far from the land, but about two hundred cubits off), dragging the net full of fishes. So when they got out upon the land, they see a fire of coals there, and fish laid thereon, and bread. Jesus saith unto them, Bring of the fish which ye have now taken. Simon Peter therefore went up, and drew the net to land, full of great fishes, a hundred and fifty and three: and for all there were so many, the net was not rent. Jesus saith unto them, Come and break your fast. And none of the disciples durst inquire of him, Who art thou? knowing that it was the Lord. Jesus cometh, and taketh the bread, and giveth them, and the fish likewise. This is now the third time that Jesus was manifested to the disciples, after that he was risen from the dead.

So when they had broken their fast, Jesus saith to Simon Peter, Simon, son of John, lovest thou me more than these? He saith unto him, Yea, Lord; thou knowest that I love thee. He saith unto him, Feed my lambs. He saith to him again a second time, Simon, son of John, lovest thou me? He saith unto him, Yea, Lord; thou knowest that I love thee. He saith unto him, Tend my sheep. He saith unto him the third time, Simon, son of John, lovest thou me? Peter was grieved because he said unto him the third time, Lovest thou me? And he said unto him, Lord, thou knowest all things; thou knowest that I love thee. Jesus saith unto him, Feed my sheep. Verily, verily, I *say unto thee, When thou wast young, thou girdest thyself, and walkedst whither thou wouldest: but when thou shalt be old, thou shalt stretch forth thy hands, and another shall gird thee, and carry thee whither thou wouldest not. Now this he spake, signifying by what manner of death he should glorify God. And when he had spoken this, he saith unto him, Follow me. Peter, turning about, seeth the disciple whom Jesus loved following; who also leaned back on his breast at the supper, and said, Lord, who is he that betrayeth thee? Peter therefore seeing him saith to Jesus, Lord, and what shall this man do? Jesus saith unto him, If I will that he tarry till I come, what is that to thee? follow thou me. This saying therefore went forth among the brethren, that that disciple should not die: yet Jesus said not unto him, that he should not die; but, If I will that he tarry till I come, what is that to thee?*

This is the disciple that beareth witness of these things, and wrote these things: and we know that his witness is true.

And there are also many other things which Jesus did, the which if they should be written every one, I suppose that even the world itself would not contain the books that should be written.

Shall we pray?

Our Lord, we do just bow here in Thy presence and we are very thankful to Thee that Thou hast promised that the Spirit of truth will lead us into truth. And Lord, we just want to ask Thee that Thou will cause that ministry of the Holy Spirit to be fulfilled in our midst.

Meet us, Lord, we pray. We ask for a spirit of quietness to come upon this gathering. Help us, Lord, to be able to attend to Thee. We don't want this time to be wasted or any way futile, but we pray that Thou wilt shut us in with Thyself, that we may hear Thee. And in hearing Thee may something be done in our hearts and lives for eternity. And we ask it in the name of our Lord Jesus. Amen.

The burden that is on my heart has been to do with the love of God. It comes out of that little word of the apostle Paul as it is recorded in his letter to the church at Philippi in chapter 1:9: "I pray that your love may abound yet more and more in knowledge and all discernment, that you may approve the things which are excellent, that you may be sincere and void of offense unto the day of Christ."

"I pray that your love may abound yet more and more." The Lord Jesus said in some of the most solemn words He uttered: "Because iniquity shall abound, the love of the many shall wax cold" (Matthew 24:12). No single believer should ever think that he will escape that category but by the grace of God. All of our hearts can grow cold. We can become lukewarm. The love that we had at the beginning may evaporate and somehow we substitute that devotion and love for the Lord with things, with work, with truths, with teachings, even with sacrifice. We need to take heed to the Lord's word in this matter. Far from waxing cold, may our love "abound yet more and more unto the day of Jesus Christ."

There is a divine challenge in this 21st chapter of John's gospel: "Lovest thou Me?" The story contained in John 21 is a very wonderful story. It is almost an epilogue, because if you look at the end of John 20, it seems as if John had finished his gospel. "Many other signs therefore did Jesus in the presence of the disciples, which are not written in this book: but these are written, that ye may believe that Jesus is the Christ, the Messiah, the Son of God; and that believing ye may have life in His name" (John 20:30–31). Then it seems as if he felt it was not finished, and the Spirit of the Lord drove him back to writing this epilogue. He wrote the epilogue, which, in fact, has become a vital part in the whole of this gospel.

I have said that we must always take note whenever God repeats something. In the Bible we have certain things which are a repetition. For instance, we saw this in Deuteronomy, the fifth book of the Old Testament, which is, in fact, a repetition of the law. It is a giving again of the law. One wonders why the Lord should have spent so much time and so many chapters in this precious book we call the Bible going over what he has already given us. There are so many things we would like revelation and illumination on, so many things we would like information on, so many questions we would like answered. Instead, it is as if God goes right back to the beginning, to Genesis, and traces the whole story again, only with a significant addition. Only once before in those four books has He spoken about this matter of His love for them lying behind everything. Therefore He is only satisfied if they will love Him with all their heart, with all their soul, with all their mind, and with all their strength.

In one way, the gospel of John is also a repetition. We call the other three gospels, Matthew, Mark, and Luke, synoptic gospels. They are the gospels which are histories. They give us the facts. They give us the story of the birth of the Lord Jesus, the life of the Lord Jesus, the anointing of the Lord Jesus, the ministry of the Lord Jesus, the death of the Lord Jesus, the resurrection of the Lord Jesus, and the ascension of the Lord Jesus. They give us the facts, and they give them from different angles. One speaks of Him as King, another speaks of Him as Servant, and the other speaks of Him as Man. But when we come to John, he speaks of Him as God, but it is not in the same way as the other gospels. He goes over the whole story again, but his gospel is an interpretation. It is as if John is saying, "Now there is something you must understand which underlies everything in these other gospels. You cannot fully understand who Jesus is and what the significance of the Lord Jesus is unless you understand what I am going to communicate to you."

So the gospel of John occupies a very special place indeed. It is as if you come into the Holy of Holies again in the gospel of John. I think most of us feel that way when we read this gospel. It is not without significance that this gospel ends with the story of the Lord Jesus and His first, foremost disciple and apostle, Peter. There are one or two things we need to say about the questions of the Lord so that we might understand.

When Peter said, "I am going fishing," Peter was just this kind of man. We do great injustice to Peter when we think of him as some impetuous, impulsive, empty-headed kind of individual. Sometimes you hear Peter described as if he were all fire and emptiness, all emotion, feeling, ready to jump in where fools fear to tread, the one who goes ahead of thought, never thinking ahead. I do not think this is true of Peter. I think Peter was a rugged man, a real he-man. He was a man who had a brain. He had not been to an academy. He was a fisherman, but he had intelligence.

He had a rugged personality, and he was as tough as they come. He was not the kind of person who was impetuous just in an empty-headed way. He was the kind of man who took the helm because it was natural for him to take the helm. He was the kind of man who spoke up because it was natural to him to speak up. He did what came naturally. He was a tough man.

In this marvelous story, we find that Jesus cooked Peter and the other disciples a meal and had breakfast with them. He suddenly said, "Simon, son of John, do you love Me more than these?" The old Peter would have said, "Lord, of course I do; much more than all of them." This is where we cannot quite put it in English because in the original we have two words used. Jesus said, "Do you love Me completely, absolutely, comprehensively, with your whole being?" And Peter said, "Lord, you know I have a brotherly affection for You." He used another word, *phileo*. It is a word beautifully used in the New Testament and with real power. We are to love the brethren fervently, it says in one place. And in other places too it uses this word, but it has not got quite the same fulness or comprehensiveness as the word Jesus used. Then the Lord Jesus said to him, "Tend My lambs."

Then He said the second time: "Simon, do you love Me with your whole being, completely?" And Simon said, "Lord, You know I have a brotherly love for You." Jesus said, "Shepherd My sheep."

And the third time Jesus said to him, "Simon, son of John (and here is the wonderful thing), have you got a brotherly affection for Me?" And Peter said, "Lord, You know everything. You know I have a brotherly affection for You." Jesus said, "Tend My sheep." This is the divine challenge.

The Mind of God Revealed

The gospel of John soars into the heavens right from the beginning. It begins just like the book of Genesis, just like the old covenant begins: "In the beginning was the Word, and the Word was with God, and the Word was God. And the Word became flesh, and dwelt among us full of grace and truth, and we beheld his glory, glory as of the only begotten of the Father" (John 1:1,14). It is a wonderful revelation of the Person of the Lord Jesus; not just the Son of Man but the Son of God; not just the Son of God, but God the Son, the very mind of God revealed.

What does it mean "a word"? A word is a thought expressed in a concrete form. What I am trying to do by the grace of God is to communicate thoughts by words. These thoughts which are in my mind are invisible and intangible. You don't see them, you can't hear them, you don't know what I am thinking. But these words take these invisible thoughts and express them in a concrete way so that you can understand. It is a communication.

Jesus is the mind of God revealed. Jesus is the heart of God revealed. Jesus is the thought of God in concrete form. Jesus is the manifestation of God so that when we see Him, we see God. When we hear Him, we hear God. When we touch Him, we touch God. He is the Word. We would never be able to understand God, comprehend God. We would never be able to taste God, if you know what I mean, apart from the Person of the Lord Jesus.

I Am the Bread of Life

Then, by the Spirit of God John begins to take us through all kinds of incredible things. First, we come to that great statement of the

Lord Jesus: "I am the bread of life." Bread is absolutely necessary to live. We have to eat bread to live. Jesus did not say, "I give you bread." He did give them bread. He broke bread and fed five thousand in one place and broke bread and fed four thousand in another place. The Bible mentions men only, but women must have been there if we go by the normal congregation—at least two-thirds more.

"I am the bread of life"; not I give the bread of life, not I break the bread of life, but I am the bread of life. He is the One who, as it were, is the very nature of God, in a way that you and I can become partakers of that divine nature. We would not be so subjective as to make Jesus a thing, but by Him, through His saving work, we become partakers of the divine nature. "I am the bread of life." What a tremendous thing it is! In this gospel, we have the story of the feeding of the five thousand and this great statement of Jesus: "I am the bread of life."

I Am the Light of the World

A little farther on we have the next great statement: "I am the light of the world. He that followeth Me shall not walk in darkness but shall have the light of life." Jesus *is* the light of the world. He does not just manifest the light of the world. He said, "I am the light of the world." And if we follow Him we shall have, not the light of knowledge, but the light of life. He in us becomes an inward understanding of God, an inward understanding of ourselves, an inward understanding of one another, an inward understanding of the purpose and goal of God. "I am the light of the world. He that followeth Me shall not walk in darkness but shall have the light of life." And we read of a blind man getting his sight.

Before Abraham Was, I Am

As we go on a little more we find this marvelous statement: "Before Abraham was, I am." They reeled back on that. How could He be before Abraham was born? But He said, "Before Abraham was, I am." It is as if He were saying, "I am the explanation of the history of God's people. I am the significance of all God's dealings with His people." "Before Abraham was, I am."

These "I Am's" in the gospel of John are amazing statements. God had revealed Himself to Moses in that burning bush as I AM. And when Moses said, "What is Your name?" God said, "I AM that I AM." And Jesus took up that unmentionable name of God and said, "I AM the bread of life; I AM the light of the world; before Abraham was, I AM."

I Am the Door

We go on for a few more chapters and we come to that wonderful tenth chapter of the gospel of John, where Jesus said, "I am the door; by Me if any man enter in, he shall be saved, and shall go in and go out, and shall find pasture" (v. 9). I am the door; not I point to the door, not I introduce you through the door, but I am the door. I am the gateway into the kingdom of God. I am the gateway into the presence of God. I am the door by which you can come in, and you can go out, and you can find pasture."

I Am the Good Shepherd

Then He went on: "I am the good Shepherd: the good Shepherd layeth down His life for the sheep" (v. 11). This gospel of John is unique. You do not find any of this in the other three gospels. It is as if John goes right back and says, "Now you have all the facts. You have seen Him as King; you have seen Him as Servant; you have seen Him as Man; but I want to reveal something about the Lord Jesus that underlies the whole. You will understand that God has not given you things; He has given you a Person. God has not given you an "it"; He has given you a "Him." His unspeakable gift is His Son. He has given Himself in the Person of the Lord Jesus.

I Am the Resurrection and the Life

Then we go on to the 11th chapter of John's gospel and we have that amazing story of when Lazarus died and Jesus wept. You remember the words He said: "I am the resurrection, and the life: he that believeth on Me, though he were dead, yet shall he live; and whosoever liveth and believeth on Me shall never die" (vv. 25-26). He did not say, "I am the one who will raise the dead and give you life." He said, "I am the resurrection and the life. He that believeth on Me, though he were dead, yet shall he live. And he that liveth and believeth" (not believeth and liveth) "on Me shall never die." Death is only a transient experience. It is just a kind of chrysalis out of which we pass into another dimension of life. Isn't that wonderful!

Jesus said, "I am the resurrection and the life." Sometimes we are afraid if we feel that Jesus is far off and I am here. But when it comes to the day we die, if the Lord does not come for us before, what a comfort it will be to know that He is the resurrection and the life even in our dying hour.

I Am the Way, the Truth, and the Life

Then you will find in the 14th chapter of John another marvelous thing. Dear Philip said, "Lord, we don't know the way to the Father; show us the way." Jesus said, "Have I been so long time with you, and you still don't understand? I am the way, the truth, and the life. No man cometh to the Father but by Me." He did not say, "I point to the way, I preach the truth or give the truth, and I produce the life." He said, "I am the way, I am the truth, I am the life. No man cometh unto the Father but by Me."

I Am the True Vine

Perhaps the most remarkable and mysterious statement of all is in John 15:1: "I am the true vine and My Father is the husbandman." Now any good Jew, hearing the Lord Jesus at that time, knew what He was talking about because on the coins at that time was stamped a vine leaf. In Herod's temple was one of the most amazing sights according to Josephus. It was the great filigree golden vine in the porch of the temple, and every child of Israel could see it when he brought his sacrifices. He looked up beyond the head of the priest to the porch of the temple and he could see that golden vine. If you had said to any good Jew in those days, "What does the vine symbolize?" he would have said, "Us; we are the vine. We who are the covenant people of God, we who are the chosen people of God, we are the vine and God is the husbandman."

Of all the things Jesus ever said that must have caused those apostles' minds to reel, the greatest was this: "I am the true vine," as if He was saying, "I am the nation; I am the people of God; I am the bride of God; I am the nation of God; I am the covenant people of God." How could He be? If He had said, "I am the Messiah of the people," we could understand it. If He had said, "I am the High Priest," we could understand it. If He had said, "I am the Messianic King," we could understand it. But how could He say, "I am the true vine"?

"I am the vine, you are the branches." He never said, "I am the trunk, you are the branches." That is how we all mentally understand it, that He is the little trunk and we are the big branches. Vines that are grown in the old way, as they still are in many parts of Israel today in Judea and Samaria, have very little trunk and great branches.

Many people say, "We understand Jesus. He said, 'I am the trunk; you are the branches. Abide in Me and you shall bear much fruit.'" He did not say that. He said, "I am the vine, you are the branches"; as if He were saying, "I am the whole vine. I am the totality of the vine. I am the root, the trunk, the branches, the leaves, the tendrils, the blossoms, and the fruit, and you are in Me. You are not as big as Me but you are in Me. Abide in Me and I in you, and you shall bear much fruit."

What a revelation! We do not realize how tremendous these things are. Here we have this gospel and many of us have never understood these things. Oh, this gospel of John is fathomless! It is an ocean of spiritual meaning and experience unexplored.

Then after that 15th chapter we enter into the last account of Jesus' passion, His anguish, His death, His burial, His resurrection. It is as if John came to the end and said, "Oh, I have written these and many other signs which I could have told you about that you might believe and that believing you might have life in His name." Then, I suppose he thought, "Well, that's it."

The Challenge of Divine Love

Then, perhaps he must have felt uncomfortable, and maybe he went back and looked at what he had written and felt there was something missing. I suppose the Lord Jesus said to him: "Yes, there is another incident. You remember when I met you all when you went fishing with Peter. John, do not leave that gospel where you finished it. It is not finished. You have not yet come to the heart of the matter. It is not that you have knowledge of all mysteries, not that you understand My person and the fulness, which the Father has pleased to center in Me for you. The key is this: 'Do you love Me? Do you love Me with *all* your heart, and *all* your soul, and *all* your mind, and your strength?'"

What is the greatest need among the people of God today? Some would say, "Oh, if they could only have more knowledge of the things of God." I think we would all say, "Yes, we wish for that." There is a dearth of understanding. But dear people of God, you can have a great understanding and still miss the mark. You could even (and no one has yet fully) understand the gospel of John and somehow miss the whole point were it not for this 21st chapter of John. It is not an afterthought but rather brings us right into the very heart of the matter: "Lovest thou Me? Do you love Me fully, completely, with your whole being?"

Just note for a moment. It is not things; it is not truths; it is not teachings. He did not say, "Do you love the truth I have given you?" It is a good thing to love the truth. The Psalmist said, "Oh Lord, I love Thy truth." It is a good thing to have sound doctrine in a day when there is very little. It is a good thing to have pure doctrine in a day when there is very little pure doctrine. But that is only part of the matter. The essential matter, the heart of the whole thing is this: "Do you love Me with all your being? And if you do, feed My lambs; tend My sheep; feed My sheep."

What are the two great commandments? "Thou shalt love the Lord thy God with all thy heart, and thou shalt love thy neighbor as thyself."

"Lovest thou Me?"

"Lord, you know I have a real affection for You."

"Feed My lambs."

Everything of eternal value comes out of our relationship to the Lord Jesus, out of our love for Him. You can have all the knowledge, all the understanding, all the zeal, all the energy, and be immersed in work for Him, but if this relationship to Him of love is missing, it profits you nothing. Nothing goes through into the city of God. There is no gold, no precious stone, and no pearl. That is why this greatest of the four gospels ends with a challenge: "Do you love Me? Tell Me. Do you love Me?" Or are you preaching out of duty, preaching mechanically, working for self-satisfaction, just simply going through the motions? "Do you love Me?"

What a revelation of the grace of God in this last chapter! He understood that apostle. The Lord Jesus could have said the third time: "Do you love Me with your whole being?" He would have known that poor Peter would have nearly gone under. Something had happened to Peter. He could not say what He would have said a few months or weeks before. He said, "Lord, You know everything."

But the third time Jesus did not say, "Do you love Me completely, fully, with your whole being?" He said, "Peter, Simon, have you got that brotherly affection for Me?" And Peter said, "Lord, you know. You know everything; you know I've got it for You." Then He said, "Feed My sheep."

The Lord Jesus comes to you with this same question. It is not your tremendous understanding of truth, even of church truth, even the purpose of God that finally counts in eternity. It is whether you can answer this question of your risen, glorified Lord: "Do you love Me?" It is an inescapable challenge.

The Consequence of Divine Love

The consequence of such love is not that we should be closeted with Him and forget the world around us or forget everybody else and somehow live in a wonderful atmosphere of meditation and reflection. The Lord says, "Feed My lambs; tend My sheep; feed My sheep." This kind of love for Him, this relationship to Him and not to things, must result in a service, a sacrificial, loving service toward the flock of God.

Sheep are not easy creatures. I knew very little about sheep before I started asking various questions of sheep farmers whenever I came into contact with them. In the Middle East we have sheep coming right through the capital twice a year. It is one of the funniest sights in Jerusalem to see in the spring and autumn whole flocks of sheep going right through the high streets on their way from the south to the north. Half a year later they would be on their way back down again to the Bethlehem area. Those scraggy old sheep are the Oriental kind, the kind they have in China as well, not the Western kind. They are the kind with the fat rump tail at the back and round faces.

Sheep are strange. I used to think they were the dumbest of all creatures, that you could do anything with a few sheep. You just sat down under a tree all through the day and let the sheep get on with it, and somehow or other, they brought you some kind of livelihood. Many people probably have considered that by keeping sheep, a person has a nice, easy way of making a subsistence livelihood. You are not making a fortune. You just have a few sheep and they go out and find their own pasture. You don't have to bother your head about them, and you can sit there playing a flute. That is the sentimental picture of a shepherd, sitting on a rock playing a flute while his sheep wander all over the mountainside. I have found out since then that sheep are not quite so easy.

A sheep farmer told me that to really have healthy sheep you must inspect them every day, personally, each one. They have such a capacity for foot rot, such a capacity for sores in their coat that they need to be inspected each day. This explains the relationship of the shepherd to the sheep. He has to inspect them every day. He gets to know them. To me the sheep all look alike, but to the shepherd he gets to know their little idiosyncrasies. He can tell one from another. I have always found this relationship of shepherd to sheep quite remarkable.

I remember one day walking from where I was staying near the Mount of Olives down into the old city. I saw a whole lot of flocks. I knew that there were four large flocks, each numbering about a hundred and fifty sheep, and they were all mixed up together. I knew there must be some way of telling them apart. One day I saw a most extraordinary sight. I saw a little short shepherd, an old white haired gentleman with an enormous sheep in his arms. He just scooped her up out of the midst of a whole seething mass of sheep and took her across and dumped her into another flock. I thought to myself: How did he know that? There was no dye on it as in modern things. How did he know that sheep was not his? Yet he sorted it out. They all looked the same to me. They all looked scraggy; they all looked silly; they all looked dumb; they all had the same color pattern; they all had the same queer face. Yet he dived into the midst of about fifteen sheep and lifted one out and put her in another flock.

Once I was down in the south of Sinai and I wandered off from the others who were looking at the coral and diving down to see the undersea water world. I walked around to where there was a Bedouin village right next to the Red Sea. There was a woman with an enormous flock and she was watering them. Then I suddenly saw her turn around and look into that seething mass of at least a hundred creatures. She bent down, took a stone and flung it with deadly aim, hitting one on the back. It jumped up and belted out of the flock and went over to another. Now I could not speak her language so I could not say, "How did you know?" To me they all looked alike, and they were all fighting to get to the water. Yet she spotted one sheep out of that hundred that was not her flock. She sent a stone with deadly accuracy and hit that sheep on the back, and out it went to its own flock.

Sheep are incredible creatures. Not only do they have a tendency to disease and have to be tended, but the shepherd has to look for pastures. It is not like here in the west where you have plenty of green grass or plenty of hay. In the Middle East the shepherd has to have foresight. He has to think where he is going to lead those sheep the next week because he knows that where they are will only enable them to live a few more days. He has to think of some other pasture.

Jesus said to Peter, who was a fisherman, "Lovest thou Me?"

Peter said, "Lord, You know I have an affection for Thee."

Jesus said, "Feed My lambs."

"Simon, do you love Me?"

"Lord, You know I have an affection for You."

"Shepherd My sheep."

"Simon, do you have an affection for Me?"

"Lord, You know everything. You know I have this affection for You."

"Feed My sheep."

Sheep have a tremendous tendency to get into trouble. I have been working among the Lord's people for some years now, and I can well understand why the Lord calls us sheep. We have a terrible tendency to disease. We have a terrible tendency to get into trouble, and sometimes we lead one another into trouble.

I remember years ago in England when I was young, hearing Alan Redpath tell a story. He was on holiday in Scotland and he said that as the ferry came into a place in the western highlands, all these sheep were coming in. They were going on to the quay, but the men on the quayside had left some great crates. As the first sheep came to the crate, it did not go around. It hesitated for a moment and then it went back and leapt over. The next one hesitated and then it leapt over. To his amazement, rather than going around the crates, all those hundreds of sheep were leaping over. Then one of the men on the quay felt sorry for the sheep and he pulled the crate away. What do you think happened? They all leapt over an invisible crate.

The Lord's people are amazing people. We follow one another; we do things, and sometimes, a hundred years later, we are following a method which is long outdated. We are doing evangelistic work as if we are living a hundred and fifty years ago. We dress like it, we speak like it, we do all kind of things as if we are living in a time of great revival that happened two hundred, three hundred, four hundred years ago. We are jumping over the invisible crate.

Now I know you are a sheep but it is sometimes hard to recognize that I am a sheep. Do you understand? We all say, "Oh, so and so is just like that; just like that. They need so much care, so much attention. But of course, me—well, I am not like that." But we all are. We are all sheep. We have all turned to our own way, but the Lord has laid the iniquity of us all on Him.

The work, the service, even the sheep must never take the place of the Lord. Isn't it interesting that the Lord Jesus did not say, "Simon, Simon, son of John, do you love My lambs?" "Simon, Simon, son of John, do you love My sheep with your whole being?" He didn't even say, "Simon, do you have a brotherly affection for the sheep, a feeling for them?" No. He said, "Do you love Me with your whole being?" "Lord, You know I have an affection for You." "Feed My lambs."

That is the right way round, but we are always putting it the other way. We are always getting wrapped up with the work, with the service, with the people, with the saints. The first thing is our relationship to the Lord Jesus. It is not for nothing that the apostle Paul said, "Hold fast the Head from whom the whole body..." In other words, when we hold fast the Head, we find the body. When we try to hold fast the body, we lose the Head. Whole movements have gone off the rails because they have held to one another instead of holding to the Head. Our great safety and security is our relationship to the Head; not just holding fast the Head but a real, true, total love for Him.

Peter's Experience

We have looked at the challenge of the Lord: "Do you love Me with your whole being?" We have looked at the consequence of that love: "Feed My lambs; tend My sheep; feed My sheep." Now we will look at the necessary experience. We must not overlook Peter's experience which lies behind all this, or we will miss the whole point. Did you notice what the Lord Jesus said to him the first time? "Simon, son of John, do you love Me more than these?" The Lord knew just what He was saying and what He was doing because the old Peter would have said, "You know, Lord. I love You far more than them all. I am ready to go with You into prison. I am ready to die for You, at least with You." That was the old Peter of a week before.

Something had happened to Peter. You see, Peter had a self-manufactured Christian life. He had a kind of self-manufactured service. He had been three years with the Lord Jesus. I cannot think of any theological seminary like that. Those three years were not under some great godly tutor, but under the tutorship and training of the Lord Jesus Himself. He had been three whole years with the Master. He had lived with Him. He had slept in the same room with Him. He had eaten with Him. He had been involved in miracles and signs and wonders. He had personally heard the Sermon on the Mount. He had heard these great discourses. He heard Jesus say, "I am the bread of life. I am the light of the world." He had been with the Lord Jesus in all these things.

Peter was the one who was up on the Mount of Transfiguration with two of the others when suddenly the Lord Jesus was transfigured in glory. He was one of the four who was taken in and saw Jairus' daughter raised from the dead. He was one of the inner circle of the twelve. He had been in on everything. He was not only with the Lord, he not only knew the Lord firsthand, he not only heard the Lord, he not only had experienced the authority and power of the Lord, he was the first with revelation. When Jesus said, "Whom do you say that I am?" he was the one who answered, "Thou art the Messiah, the Son of the living God." And Jesus said to him: "Simon, son of John, flesh and blood did not reveal that to you but My Father who is in heaven." He was the first in revelation. It was to Peter that Jesus said, "To you will I give the keys of the kingdom of heaven." Peter had been on evangelistic campaigns and when they came back, Jesus said to them: "I saw Satan falling out of the heavens like lightning." They came back and they said, "Master, the dead have been raised, the lepers have been cleansed, the sick have been healed, the demon possessed have been made sound."

I would have thought that if you had had three years like that you might feel that you had a right to speak for God. You might feel you had a right to be a leader amongst the people of God. You might feel that you had a right to communicate truth to them. You might feel that you had a right to somehow organize campaigns or whatever, but there was a fatal weakness in Peter. And that fatal weakness is in every single child of God. We find it best described in Luke 22:31 in the words of Jesus: "'Simon, Simon, behold, Satan asked to have you, that he might sift you as wheat: but I have prayed for thee, that thy faith fail not; and do thou, when once thou hast turned again, establish thy brethren.' And he said unto him, 'Lord, with Thee I am ready to go both to prison and to death.' And He said, 'I tell thee, Peter, the cock shall not crow this day, until thou shalt thrice deny that thou even knowest Me.'"

"Simon, Satan has obtained thee by request." The New American Standard Bible puts it simply: "Satan has demanded permission to have you." What a wonderful word! So Satan can never get a believer without permission. No one who has been given by the Father to the Son can ever be tampered with by Satan but by permission. And what was the aim? "Satan has demanded permission that he might have you that he may sift you as wheat."

I think God always uses Satan to sift us. In many, many ways it is Satan who is the agent. God gets the grain; Satan gets the chaff. And Satan is so self-centered that he still goes on and on and on and on. He does not seem to realize that God uses him to do something in a believer.

"Satan hath obtained thee by request that he may sift thee as wheat." Now I would have thought that if we take the story of Peter's denial and collapse, there was no grain. It was all chaff. Everything was chaff. He said with oaths and curses: "I do not know this Man." And it was not before the high priest he said it. I might have understood it if the high priest appeared in all his regalia and confronted Peter and said, "You have been with this imposter, Jesus," and Peter had quivered and said, "Oh, I do not know Him." But it was a little servant girl, who came up and said, "You were with Jesus." And that great rugged man quaked. He said, "I do not know Him" three times.

Divine Love in Action

Here is divine love in action: "I have prayed for you that your faith fail not." Do you know why I stand here tonight? Because Jesus has prayed for me many times. Do you know why you are here tonight? Because He ever lives to make intercession for us. Oh, the times unbeknown to us when Jesus has said to the Father: "Father, do not let her faith fail. Do not let that which is of Myself in him be destroyed. Bring him through with what is of eternal value. The rest Satan can have."

How would you have described this chapter in Peter's life? Wouldn't you have called it the collapse of his faith? I would have thought if someone had said, "I do not know the Man," with oaths and curses, it would have been the collapse of his faith. Not the Lord Jesus. He said, "I prayed for you, Simon, that your faith would not fail." All that failed was the superficial, self-manufactured stuff. It was the surface stuff. The real faith which is the gift of God deep within his heart was there. It never failed. Jesus only had to look at him with one glance, and in that moment his God-given faith broke out in bitter tears.

So it is with every true child of God. Jesus has only to look. Sometimes He does not even have to say anything. When we have gone through this kind of experience, He looks, and in that moment we are back with Him.

What happened to Peter has to happen to every true servant of the Lord in some degree. When we are first saved, we all start out to serve the Lord, but so much of it is self-manufactured, isn't it? Our faith which we think is so great is really superficial. Our confession is: "Lord, I will go anywhere for You. Lord, I will do anything." We stand up in meetings and dedicate ourselves to the Lord, but the Lord is not taken in by any of it. He loves us so much that He takes us on. It is as if He plays along with us and says, "Okay, okay, I take you." But He knows, just like He knew Peter.

He did not say to Peter every time Peter said something, "Peter, you are all wind; empty, noisy gong, clanging cymbal. That is all you are. You will come to it." No, the Lord Jesus went along. He encouraged what there was of the Lord. He said, "Flesh and blood did not reveal that to you. My Father revealed that to you." He commended him; He encouraged him; He comforted him. Sometimes He rebuked him: "Get thee behind Me, Satan. You do not savor the things which are of God but the things which are of men." The Lord Jesus was never taken in. He knew all that so-called Christian character and Christian work and service was all a façade. It would all collapse in a moment of time; and He had prayed for Peter that he would not fail.

If you go on with the Lord, you will have to come to this in some degree, but some of you may have already come to this place. Seemingly, you have lost your faith. Seemingly, you are devastated. Seemingly, you are desolated. All that you once knew has just evaporated. All that you once held so zealously and forcefully has somehow got a question about it. It is as if God has blown the whole superstructure of your Christian life to pieces. Do not be afraid. Jesus has prayed for you. You have got to go this way because only when you have come through will you hear the lovely words of your Lord: "Do you love Me with your whole being?"

If Jesus had said that to Peter earlier, he would have said, "Of course I do, Lord. I love You with my whole being. I will die for You." Jesus would have known it did not mean a thing. Now He said it twice. And those words of Peter, "You know I have an affection for You, Lord," meant more to Jesus than if he had said in months before: "I love You with my whole heart." This time Jesus knew it was real. The man was in love with Him. The man had a devotion for Him, but he was afraid to go beyond and use the words that he would have used a few weeks before. His whole superstructure was blown sky high. God had gotten him down to basic foundations: "You know I have an affection for You."

Jesus did not let him get away. "Simon, do you love Me with your whole heart?" "Master, You know I have an affection for You." "Shepherd My sheep." Then it was as if Jesus said with a gentleness and a tenderness in His eye: "Simon, do you have an affection for Me?" And Peter said, "You know everything; You know I have an affection for You." And Jesus said, "Feed My sheep. I am with you, Peter. We are on the basis of reality now. You are going to be the man who opens the door, first to the Jew and then to the Gentile. I am with you."

Oh, dear people of God, isn't it an amazing thing when we consider that this love of God has to lead us in the end to laying down our lives for Him and for one another? Do you notice how the words end? "Do you love Me? Follow Me."

It was not for nothing that Jesus said to him, "You will be carried where you would not." For He spoke of Peter dying a death that was actually, physically like his Lord's. If we believe church tradition, at the last moment Peter asked for one thing to be granted to him, and it was granted to him. He said he wanted to be crucified upside down because he was not worthy to be crucified in the same way as his Lord.

"Follow Me." You can give your body to be burned and it will profit you nothing. You can give all your goods away to feed the poor and it means nothing unless there is love. "Do you love Me?" the Lord says. "Lord, You know I love You." Then He says, "Feed My sheep and follow Me." That will mean you will have to lay down your life. And the love of God leads us to do just that, that we might lay down our lives for Him and for one another.

I do not know what the response of your heart is to the words of Jesus. I pray that you cannot escape it, that God will somehow keep you to this matter. It is not: do you understand? It is not: do you know? It is not: are you ready to sacrifice first? It is not even: are you ready to serve first? It is: do you love Me? May God give us grace to love Him with all our heart and with all our soul and with all our mind and with all our strength and to love our neighbor as ourselves.

Shall we pray?

Dear Lord, we pray that we may hear Thy voice speaking to each one of us in the quietness of our own heart. Help us, Lord, we pray to respond to Thee. Don't let us escape we pray, Lord, from this challenge of Thine, but grant that we may be enabled to face up to it and may be enabled to seek Thee. We ask it in the name of our Lord Jesus. Amen.

3.
The Divine Diagnosis

Revelation 2:1–7

To the angel of the church in Ephesus write: These things saith he that holdeth the seven stars in his right hand, he that walketh in the midst of the seven golden candlesticks: I know thy works, and thy toil and patience, and that thou canst not bear evil men, and didst try them that call themselves apostles, and they are not, and didst find them false; and thou hast patience and didst bear for my name's sake, and hast not grown weary. But I have this against thee, that thou didst leave thy first love. Remember therefore whence thou art fallen, and repent and do the first works; or else I come to thee, and will move thy candlestick out of its place, except thou repent. But this thou hast, that thou hatest the works of the Nicolaitans, which I also hate. He that hath an ear, let him hear what the Spirit saith to the churches. To him that overcometh, to him will I give to eat of the tree of life, which is in the Paradise of God.

Revelation 3:14–22

And to the angel of the church in Laodicea write: These things saith the Amen, the faithful and true witness, the beginning of the creation of God: I know thy works, that thou art neither cold nor hot: I would thou wert cold or hot. So because thou art lukewarm, and neither hot nor cold, I will spew thee out of my mouth. Because thou sayest, I am rich, and have gotten riches, and have need of nothing; and knowest not that thou art the wretched one and miserable and poor and blind and naked: I counsel thee to buy of me gold refined by fire, that thou mayest become rich; and white garments, that thou mayest clothe thyself, and that the shame of thy nakedness be not made manifest; and eyesalve to anoint thine eyes, that thou mayest see. As many as I love, I reprove and chasten: be zealous therefore, and repent. Behold, I stand at the door and knock: if any man hear my voice and open the door, I will come in to him, and will sup with him, and he with me. He that overcometh, I will give to him to sit down with me in my throne, as I also overcame, and sat down with my Father in his throne. He that hath an ear, let him hear what the Spirit saith to the churches.

Shall we pray?

Dear Lord, we do want to thank Thee that Thou art here in our midst and that we are gathering together unto Thee. We want to ask, Lord, as we come to Thy word that Thou wilt take Thy word and make it live to us. Deliver us from somehow bypassing Thy word or

There have been a tremendous number of books written on the book of Revelation, and I have often felt that the more you read the books on Revelation the more muddled and confused you become. Sometimes you feel like putting an ice pack on your head and then going back to the book of Revelation for relief. There are so many conflicting, complex theories that are built upon this book of Revelation. I cannot help feeling that some of it is because it is taken as if it is independent of all the other books of the Bible. But you cannot really understand the book of Revelation (not that I claim to understand it fully at all) without an understanding, for instance, of Daniel, of Ezekiel, of Joel, and of Zechariah. You have to really understand and know these four books before you can come to the book of Revelation because it draws from these books. The pictures that we find in the book of Revelation are drawn from other pictures that were previously given to these prophets.

The book of Revelation has come by divine ordination to be the final book of the canon of Scripture. It is an interesting fact that until the fourth century it occupied different places. Sometimes it was attached to the book of Acts, sometimes to the gospels. It was questioned until the fourth century by many as to whether it should be in the canon. Finally, God brought it to the place it ought to occupy, the last book of the sixty-six books of the Bible. The wonderful thing about this book of Revelation is that it covers the whole of our life.

John the apostle was imprisoned on the isle of Patmos in a forced labor camp. He was a political detainee. He was being worked to death. It was the policy of the Roman Empire that if there were people who were dangerous politically, they put them away and worked them to death. It was like the Nazi concentration camp over which used to be written: "Work frees you." The idea was that by working those people to death they produced some value for the empire, and got rid of political problems and dangers.

We don't really know why, but John, the apostle, was imprisoned on the isle of Patmos in such a forced labor camp. It was the last place on earth you would ever expect a man to have visions. Most people think that if you are going to get a vision you need to go up some glorious mountainside, away from all the noise and bustle of the city and all the problems of daily life. There you sit with glorious views, marvelous sunrises, glorious sunsets, and twittering birds. Then suddenly, God shows you all kinds of things. But God does not do it this way. He gave some of the greatest revelations that have ever been committed to human beings to a man who was chained to a soldier. There he sat, dictating letter after letter after letter, which have come to us to be almost the high water mark of revelation. I think of Ephesians, of Colossians, and Philippians—those marvelous letters of the apostle Paul. They were not written in some wonderful retreat. They were written under house arrest, written with a Roman soldier chained to him day and night, written under the most adverse and contrary conditions.

It was so with John the apostle. What he was doing we do not know; whether he was working or not, we do not know either. But on a certain day that he called the Lord's Day (whether it was Sunday or whether it was the day of the Lord, we are not absolutely sure; it does not really matter) he suddenly heard a voice behind him. And turning around he saw seven golden lampstands alight. And in the midst of the seven golden lampstands, he saw the risen, glorified, ascended Messiah. Then he was told: "Write these messages." One after another, the Lord Jesus gave to John a message for seven churches, all in what we call Asia Minor.

After that, John saw vision after vision after vision after vision. These visions were horrific in some ways and glorious in other ways. He saw dragons, and serpents, and beasts, and false prophets, and martyrdom, and persecution. He saw worldwide antichristian systems not allowing selling or buying unless you were registered with them. He saw the nations of the world brought together. He saw a world government emerging. He saw a great prostitute riding on the beast. He saw the Lamb standing on Mount Zion and a hundred and forty-four thousand sealed with a seal in their foreheads. He saw all the martyrs under the altar of God crying out: "How long, oh Lord, before Thou does avenge us?" He saw that great sign in the heavens, a woman giving birth to a manchild, who, as he was born, was caught up to heaven so that the dragon could not swallow him. What amazing visions this man saw! These visions have intrigued and perplexed and often divided believers down through the years. The visions ended with the destruction of the whole anti-God, anti-Christ system, and the dynamic and spirit of that whole system, Satan himself, thrown into a bottomless abyss. Then he saw coming out of heaven the New Jerusalem, adorned as a bride for her husband.

The Seven Golden Lampstands

What does all this have to say to us? It has quite a lot. First of all, I would just like to note one wonderful thing. Whatever we may feel about the prophetic interpretation of the book of Revelation, one thing seems to me reasonably clear. The first three chapters and the last two chapters correspond in the most remarkable way. In the midst of those seven golden lampstands was the risen Christ. We are told expressly in Revelation 1:20 that those lampstands represented seven local churches, and we are given the names of the seven local churches. There are people who believe that they represent different stages of church history, and I find that a very, fascinating and instructive interpretation. I have often felt that the book of Revelation permits a number of interpretations which are valid. I find that quite remarkable. Only the word of God could do that. It is like a diamond. You turn it different ways and it flashes different colors, different lights from its different facets. You cannot do that with Shakespeare; you cannot do that with Goethe; you cannot do that with Mark Twain. You cannot do that with ordinary literature even when it is the work of genius, but with the Bible, it is quite remarkable.

Now, there are those who believe the seven churches represent different phases in church history, which is a fascinating and instructive interpretation. But I cannot help feeling that although it is valid, the basic interpretation has to be that you have seven churches that were selected to represent the whole church of God in time, on earth, and in given places. These were not church by name; these were real churches. They had all the problems of the church down here on earth, all the immorality, all the division, all the false teaching, all the faction, all the lukewarmness, all the many problems that beset us. But these seven churches were selected to represent the whole church of God in time, on earth, in given localities, in given places.

The risen Lord in the midst speaks to each church. He encourages them, He comforts them, He strengthens them, He corrects them, He rebukes them, and He warns them. And to each church He ends in the same way: "To him that overcomes will I grant this or that or the other. He that has an ear, let him hear what the Spirit says to the churches."

When we come to the last two chapters of the Bible, the scene has changed. It is no longer the church on earth, in time, in given places. Now suddenly we are looking into eternity. We find a most wonderful thing in Revelation 21:23: "And the city hath no need of the sun, neither of the moon, to shine upon it: for the glory of God did lighten it, and the lamp thereof is the Lamb." The old version used to say candlestick, which is a very unfortunate translation because it is lampstand. I think it has been corrected in the modern versions.

A lampstand has a stand and has a lamp that fits into the top of it. The menorah, the seven-branched lampstand that was in the temple, had seven branches and on the top of each one was fitted a lamp. When John saw those seven golden lampstands, he saw exactly that, not candlesticks but lampstands. When John saw the city coming down out of heaven having the glory of God, he heard this word: "It has no need of sun or moon to lighten it, for the glory of God lightens it, and the Lamb is the light thereof." The seven-fold lamp is the Lamb.

What is the stand? The city is the stand. So you have at the end of the book of Revelation the lampstand again. Only this time it is not to do with the earth and with time and with locality or place; it is to do with eternity.

To Him that Overcometh

Then you find the same word, "To him that overcometh," in Revelation 21:6-7. "And he said unto me, They are come to pass. I am the Alpha and the Omega, the beginning and the end. I will give unto him that is athirst of the fountain of the water of life freely. He that overcometh shall inherit these things; and I will be his God, and he shall be my son"—not My child, but My son. It is as if God is saying, "I want someone who is not a baby but has grown up from childhood to be My son, that he may inherit these things and administer these things." You have the same word about hearing in chapter 22:17: "And the Spirit and the bride say, Come. And he that heareth, let him say, Come."

Surely this correspondence between the last chapters and the first chapters is no coincidence. Here we have something that spans the whole book of Revelation and all the complex and mysterious visions that are contained within it. And surely it must have tremendous bearing upon all of us. What the Lord is trying to say as He depicts the whole scene that we shall pass through in this age is this: "The key to the whole thing is not just being saved and not just serving the Lord. It is being involved in the building of His church." That is the key to the whole age. It is the key to the ages of time. It is as if God is saying to us all: "Don't just look upon those last visions in the Bible as wonderful, glorious ideals and pictures. If you are going to be part of that bride, if you are going to come to reign with Christ forever and ever, if you are going to come to His throne to be with Him and to sit with Him in His throne, then you have got to be involved in all that He is doing on earth, in time and place with other brothers and sisters.

The Bride and the City

What is the divine goal? The divine goal is a bride, a city. What an extraordinary combination of contrary matters this is! You do not normally think of a bride and a city as having a relationship. No man speaks of his wife as "my city." The President would not think of speaking of Washington D.C. as "my bride." It doesn't make sense, does it? We are all used to it because it is in the Bible.

Some people say this city is a literal city. I have no doubt that there will be a city because there will be a new heaven and a new earth wherein dwells righteousness. And the headquarters of God are going to be located somewhere. If there are going to be nations, if there is going to be righteousness from end to end of the earth, if the knowledge of the glory of God is going to cover the earth as the waters cover the sea, somewhere there is going to be a capital, a hub of administration, the center of everything. So I don't doubt that there is a city somewhere. But what I have to question is whether the city that we have in Revelation 21 and 22 is to be taken literally as a city in the first place.

If you look very carefully at this city it is an extraordinary city. It is as long as it is broad as it is high. That is quite extraordinary. For it to be 1,800 miles long and broad is one thing, but for it to be 1,800 miles high is another. Now I know in this country you do build high, but even you haven't got up to that yet. I have no doubt they have plans for possibly sometime doing something somewhere up in space (God forbid). But I do not think that is what this city is talking about because it only has one street. We sing hymns that say we are going to tread the golden streets, but there is no such thing as golden streets. There is only one golden street. How do you get one street in a city so immense and so high, unless it is a spiral and somehow goes into all the gates as you go up? It does not make sense, does it?

Then it is transparent as glass. Who wants to live in a city transparent as glass? It is bad enough having your friends in and out all the time, but to live in a house which is glass, so that people can see clean through it and you can see everybody else and everything they do is amazing. I know we shall be different in those days, but still I would have thought privacy is part of something to do with man and woman.

You have never heard of a city that is produced out of gold and precious stone and pearl. That is a sure sign there cannot be any crime anywhere or they would be hacking it to pieces. You could not have such a city. Now taking all these things into consideration we have to come to a conclusion. The conclusion is that we have a spiritual reality, a spiritual entity, an eternal reality represented by these wonderful symbols. A bride represents the most intimate love and union known to mankind. A city represents administration and commerce. A capital city represents the central administration for a whole nation and empire.

Have Dominion

Now in the most incredible way, when you come to the end of the Bible, God brings two things together which were there in Genesis. He said to man: "Have dominion, subdue the earth, replenish it, rule it." Then He put him in a garden and said, "Keep and guard this garden." If only man had not failed,

God would have said that it was time to add an allotment to the garden, and another allotment to the garden, and another allotment to the garden. Slowly, man would have moved out from the garden to subdue the whole earth. It was not that it was necessarily sin in the earth which required it be subdued, as some believe. It could just be that life is riot. Remember that. You cannot have life so that every single thing goes well. Life has to be trained, it has to be pruned, it has to be disciplined. And when God said, "Let the living things be," they all began to grow everywhere, wildly, in a great riot. We know that there was not the same amount of weeds and thistles and thorns as there was later because that came in with the curse. Nevertheless, there was a riot of life and man was to subdue it; but he failed. If only he had won, wouldn't it have been an amazing thing? One of the first things God ever said to man was: "Have dominion." And that is one of the themes of the Bible.

Why did God create us? God created us that we might reign. God created us that we might learn how to have dominion. God created us that in union with Himself we might learn first in the kindergarten of Paradise, the kindergarten of Eden, the elementary, fundamental lessons. Then we would have moved on to learn more if man had not fallen, and at some point man would have been transfigured in glory. He would have obtained the glory of God. He would have succeeded instead of failing. He would have been like Jesus on the mount of Transfiguration. It was not a spotlight coming out of an open heaven shining on Him, causing everything to be seen clearly, but something happened inside of Him as a Man. His whole skin and body radiated glory so that His clothes were transfigured and His flesh was transfigured. It was like the sun being switched on inside of Him.

Do you know that is what you were made for? Only we sinned and fell short of the glory of God. That is what we are destined for. Isn't that wonderful? If we had gone on, God would have said, "Now there is more to subdue and more to administer. You must learn not only to conquer the earth, subdue the earth, have dominion over the earth and over the wild beasts of the earth as well as domestic animals of the earth, but you must learn *now.*"

Wouldn't it have been wonderful to have had that experience that Joy Adamson had with *Born Free*? That is what we were born for. We should have been able to pet a lion and speak to a tiger and say to an elephant: "More firewood." That is what we should have had in the kindergarten at the beginning. We were to have dominion over the wild beasts as well as the domestic animals and then God would have said, "Now you can go into a new dimension, a spiritual dimension. You must learn to rule in the invisible, where there are invisible thrones and powers. You must learn to reign there. What a tremendous thing! But man fell. All through the Bible you have this theme of government. All through the Bible you have this theme of dominion. All through the Bible you have this theme of authority. All through the Bible you have this theme of kingship.

Man fell, but God sent His only begotten Son to save us and to bring us back into His original purpose. So what is God doing with us? He is seeking to make us kings and priests unto Him. Jesus said, "To him that overcometh will I grant to sit down with me in My throne even as I also overcame and sat down with My Father in His throne."

The Bride

The other thing you have right through the Bible is this matter of the bride. In the second chapter of Genesis you have the story of the institution of human marriage. And we know from the way God speaks about it later that this was instituted to represent the spiritual reality that He was looking for and for which we human beings were created. Marriage is only until death do us part, but this marriage that God's speaks of is forever. Marriage was instituted for time, but this marriage between the Lamb and the wife of the Lamb is for eternity.

As you go through the Bible, you see it again and again and again. But when we come to the end of the Bible, we find that the bride is a city and the wife of the Lamb is the New Jerusalem. These two themes are brought together. You have the most intimate loving relationship and union known to mankind, only in a spiritual way forever between God and His own, between Christ and His bride. Not only that, you also have that city which is to be the eternal center of God's administration for all the ages to come. We do not even know what God is going to do in the ages to come. We do not know whether there will be new universes. When God has filled this universe with His glory, He might say to us, "I think we will create another universe with sort of new principles." Of course, we have to be very careful because it is all speculation.

God's Plan for Eternity

Some people seem to think that God has exhausted Himself. Don't pray too much to God; he gave you intelligence. He is old and He has to lie down in the afternoon. You must not bother Him too much. He has got too much on His mind already with all of these millions of people all asking Him things. Don't you come with your little problems.

Isn't that the way, subconsciously, we think of God, that somehow or other He is worn out, tired, and this world has really taken it out of Him? He put every single thing He had into this world, and now He is quite exhausted because He would not give up. He has persevered with us but He is just about to come to the end. So when finally sin is finished with and Satan is finished with and there is a new heaven and new earth, it is as if God says, "Well, I haven't got any more to do; I cannot do anymore. I have exhausted everything." It is nonsense! Nonsense! God hasn't started yet. You just wait. People get so excited with these pictures of Mars. They like to see the other side of Venus and Mars, and all it looks like is some moonscape. I cannot think of anything any more ghastly. This wonderful planet that God has created has an infinite and delicate balance in which only within this little area can the life that we know exist. It is incredible. Do you think that God has exhausted everything? Never! Never! Never! Even this universe has only a pale reflection of what God originally intended for it.

One day, as the apostle Paul said in Romans 8, when that bondage to corruption is finally broken, then somehow things will all be transformed. What does it all mean? We only know that the prophets speak about lions lying down with lambs, and children playing with adders and asps, and bears and kids feeding on straw together. It is an amazing picture. It has to be in Sunday School language so that we can take it in, but that is only the beginning.

Do you think that God is just going to have us forever and ever and ever looking at these animals eating straw with one another and some child playing with an adder? And then He will say, "I think we have had enough of that; now we will have a thousand years of hallelujah chorus." So we all go in and we all sing a hallelujah chorus for a thousand years, and then He says, "Now go out and have another look at the animals." So we all go out and have another look. The child plays with the adder again and we see the bear and the kid eating straw. It is so nonsensical. No wonder people laugh at us. They say what a boring eternity those Christians are going to have. They are pretty dull anyway. They are all going to be up there forever and ever and ever boring one another to death. Now I know that the best among us will say that the Lord is so glorious and so beautiful that just to look at Him will be satisfying and fulfilling. But God is not proud. God does not just stand there and say, "I want to be admired with all of you standing around Me and forever telling Me how wonderful I am." God is not like that. God (may I say it reverently) is inherent genius. The genius in mankind is the palest reflection of the divine genius. God has been inhibited by the fall if you know what I mean. (I wrestle with human language.) He has been inhibited in what He wanted to do. So we have a parenthesis of sin and time, but one day that whole parenthesis will be over. The first and former things will have gone forever, and then God will turn around and say, "Now My bride, let's get on with it. Let's go out into the ages and reign together in glory."

The On-High Calling

Well, dear folks, I think it is worth being saved to be in that. There has been a little bit of affliction here, and a little bit of suffering here, and a few bad circumstances, and a few inexplicable problems. Quite honestly, when we are there we will laugh about it. You just wait. I will have you to tea and we will sit down and have a good laugh. I will say, "You remember that inexplicable problem that you spent so much time crying over? Look what it has done— radiating glory! You will hardly be able to talk.

You will say it was worth it. Oh, the love of God that gave me that problem, the love of God that brought that inexplicable thing into my circumstances! You will not say, "Oh, how can a loving God do this?" You will say, "Oh, it was the love of God. I see it now. It was the love of God. It was a pinprick of time and He brought all that into my experience and He pressed me almost beyond measure, and He drove me to Himself. But I found out His love for me and I began to love Him. Oh, I cannot tell you how thankful I am for every single thing that He did. It has brought me to the throne. It has brought me into the bride. It has brought me into a union with the Lamb which is forever and ever.

I feel sorry for Christians that are filled with bitterness and distrust. They think God is some Victorian grandfather who hates them, who loves for them to be miserable, who will pile problems upon them. If you look at time, of course it is like that, but if God shows you an eternal horizon, suddenly it is light affliction which is but for a moment. This light affliction works for us an exceeding and eternal weight of glory; while we look not at the things which are seen, for the things which are seen are temporal, but we look at the things which are not seen, for the things which are not seen are eternal (see II Corinthians 4:17–18).

This book of Revelation is the most precious book in the Bible. It may be the most mysterious book and the most complex book, but it is surely the most precious. That is why it says at the end, "Everyone who reads this book will get a blessing." I know many people who have not gotten a blessing, and in fact they have come to me and said, "This blessing certainly escaped me. I got so worked up, almost to a spiritual neurosis over this book. I cannot understand it—trumpets, bowls, plagues, vials, seals. I just do not understand it. Where is the blessing?"

I'll tell you where the blessing is. It is in an understanding of the profound simplicity of the book of Revelation. Forget for a moment the complexity of the mystery and think of the bride and the city. Oh, what profound simplicity! The whole Bible is a love story. God loves you. He does not want one of those bureaucratic, eternal, civil services where people sit behind computers, and tap them like machines with mask-like, human-less faces. They give you a form to fill in, stamp something on it, and give it back to you. That is how we think of this administration.

God says, "Don't you think of My administration like that. I do not want anything to do with that kind of administration. I want an administration that comes out of love. They have loved the Lord their God with all their heart, with all their soul, with all their mind, and with all their strength, and they have loved their neighbor as themselves. They have laid down their lives as I laid down My life. They have followed Me the whole way, and now I want to bring them into a union with Myself which is an intimate, eternal, personal, direct union in which they belong to Me. They are My bride; they are My wife; they are My family; they are Me; and together we will reign from the throne of God."

Dear people of God, I think that is something worth considering. No wonder the Bible says that you have such a high calling. Did you know it? Did you know that God has saved you with this calling in view? It is something so tremendous. He wants to bring you to the throne. Only He does not want to bring you to the throne in a kind of dutiful manner, a kind of mechanical manner. He wants to bring you to the throne by the way of love.

Do you see the divine goal? The divine goal is this wife of the Lamb, this bride of Christ. What the aim of God is in the ages to come, I don't know. Does anybody? What the Lord is going to do in the ages to come, He knows. It is enough for me to know that He wants me to be in a bridal relationship to Him. That is how the Bible ends, with a marriage. The two go out into the ages to come, united, married, a divine home set up, and from that home there will be a government that will administer the will of God and the kingdom of God. That is enough for me. I know just enough of the Lord to know that all of His ways are wonderful and all His ways are grace. I cannot think of anything more wonderful than the ages to come in which we shall forever be seeing the works of God and the ways of God—fathomless, inexplorable. Oh, glory!

The Sphere of Our Practical Involvement

Now, the sphere of our practical involvement in this bride, this city, is tied to those seven golden lampstands in the first three chapters of the book of Revelation. It is as if the Lord is saying, "Don't think you can just sort of float through life, that you can just somehow go through with unsettled issues. You never know anything of spiritual discipline or authority. You never know anything of submitting to fellowship. You never know what it is to be built one to another. You never know what it is to submit one to another. You never know what it is to go through together."

It would be a wonderful thing in many people's eyes if God could wave a kind of magic wand as in a fairy tale and suddenly say, "Let all these difficult Christians be made perfect." And then suddenly, in a flash, we are all wonderful. Human personality is not like that. If I may so speak in human terms: God took the greatest risk that He ever took when He created man because He created man, spirit, soul, and body. And in creating human personalities, God created something so beautiful, so complex, and when it goes wrong, so diabolical.

It takes a lot of training, a lot of discipline, a lot of education to bring fallen men and women, saved by His grace, born of His Spirit, through the school of Christ to the place where they can reign with Him and be His bride. God is being very careful about this matter. I have no doubt that it is one of the reasons why He deals in the way He does with some of His choicest servants. He takes an apostle Paul, whom we could well have had down here longer and have written a few more letters, but at the early age of sixty-six he is martyred. Think what more we could have obtained. We would have kept him; God takes him.

God takes a Watchman Nee and puts him in prison for twenty years only to die at the end of it. What a waste! Why does He do it? I can think of many of us who could well have done with a spell inside alongside our brother. It might have cured us of a lot of things. We could have done with brother Nee's ministry, his counsel, his fellowship. But not God. You see, God has special candidates for special positions, and God brings into those lives all kinds of things because in the end He is carefully training and educating for an eternal vocation. He will therefore sometimes take us out of the running and put us aside. Sometimes He will do exactly what He has done with our brother or with others in different ways, but it adds up to the same thing because He is training with an eternal vocation in mind.

Dear brothers and sisters, this matter of the church down here is very, very important. It is all-important. Do you notice that to every one of those real churches, in spite of all their sordidness and problems, God speaks "to him that overcomes." Some people do not like any teaching on overcomers. They say it is a kind of separatism; it is an elitism; we are making a kind of elite group. Yes, I understand that; if we are going to talk about some kind of elite group who know that they are overcomers and the rest are not, I think it is very, very wrong indeed. But I remember Mr. Sparks once called overcomers "the advanced working party." For me that delivered the whole idea from elitism and put it into its proper perspective. God takes people who will give Him everything and He takes them right the way through and pioneers a way by them. It is like Joseph who went down into Egypt and then the rest of the brothers came into the blessing. It is not elitism, but it is training. Now do you begin to see something?

This matter of love is essential. No man, no woman will be an overcomer except by divine love. You will count the cost and fall out. You will find the sacrifice too much, the warfare too fierce, the problems too inexplicable. You will fall out. It is only those who have first love that will ever be overcomers. A lukewarm Christian will never be an overcomer, not in a million, million years. You can have an understanding of the Bible so that you can write theological treatises on it, you can have an understanding of the purpose of God so that you can preach from now until next week on the eternal purpose of God, you can have a knowledge of church truth in which you can distinguish the things that differ and put everything into its place, but if you do not have first love you will never be an overcomer. You will never come to that throne of His to reign with Him. You will be saved, you will be in the kingdom, but you will not reign with Him. For if we do not suffer with Him, we shall not reign with Him the Book says.

First Love

Do you see what I meant when I entitled this message "The Divine Diagnosis"? You are probably wondering why I didn't call it the divine goal because that is what I have been talking about. Ah, just wait. I do not want to leave you with the divine goal. Too many of you know something about the divine goal. That is not what I want to emphasize and underline. What I want to underline is the "Divine Diagnosis."

In the beginning of the book of Revelation are these messages to the seven churches, which represent the whole church in time, on earth, in given places. The first message to the first church is to do with love and the last message to the last church is about love. We cannot escape that.

"I have this against you, that you have left your first love. Repent therefore, and do the first works; or else I will come and remove your lampstand out of its place, except you repent" (see Revelation 2:4,5).

"I know your works, that you are neither hot nor cold: I would that you were either hot or cold, but you are lukewarm; therefore I will spew you out of My mouth" (see Revelation 3:15–16).

Ephesus was a church, which, when compared with other churches, was marvelous. The Lord had this to say about it: "I know thy works, and thy toil and patience, and that thou canst not bear evil men, and didst try them that call themselves apostles, and they are not, and didst find them false" (good discernment); "and thou hast patience and didst bear for my name's sake" (what a beautiful thing; they endured), "and hast not grown weary." And He says, "But this thou hast, that thou hatest the works of the Nicolaitans, which I also hate" (Revelation 2:2, 3, 6).

That is some commendation. I would say that if we were to judge the normal fellowship of God's people, the normal community of God's people by this standard, many of them would come off well. We would say, "Well, here we are. We have reasonably good standards here." I think most of us would be very happy if the churches we were in came up to this standard: work of God, toil for God, patience in adversity and problems, discernment over error and false teaching and false leaders, endurance and not growing weary. I think that is some commendation. Yet in spite of it all the Lord says, "No, I will be through with this thing. I will turn My back on it. It is a sham. They have left their first love."

Dear child of God, do you think the Lord might say that of you? Could He be saying it of me? Could He be saying it of us? Why is He seemingly so harsh? Why? It is because He loves so much. He has loved you and me so much, He has given so much for us that He cannot bear anything to be substituted for love. Love demands love. Love requires love. There is no other alternative. You cannot satisfy someone who loves you with work and toil and patience and discernment and good judgment. It is obnoxious! If a person loves you, they want your love first and then those other things. Otherwise, if it is a substitute for your love, it becomes something that pains them, grieves them, quenches them, makes them sick.

The Lukewarm Church

Oh, the lukewarmness of present day Christianity! How comfortable we are, how affluent we are! We have our routine. We go twice a day on Sunday and once in the week. Isn't that enough in our busy lives? Please don't disturb us. We have to work it all out. We've got to organize ourselves.

But God says, "I wish that you were cold." What a thing for God to say to the church at Laodicea: "I wish you were cold. This lukewarmness I hate. I wish you were either white hot or frozen solid. But this lukewarmness I cannot bear." And He uses a word in Greek which is really dreadful. He says, "I will vomit you out." It is so vulgar. That is what it has brought the Lord to. He does not spare words. He does not use nice words, even though the King James puts it rather nicely. But if you think of Him spewing you out, it is not a very nice word, is it? What a thing for the Lord to say to a believer: "You make Me sick." That is exactly what it says in one of the modern versions: "You make Me sick; I shall vomit you out."

Some of you may be quite shocked when you hear a person like me saying this. You may be thinking: Well, I didn't come to hear that kind of thing. That is not nice. But don't have an argument with me; you have an argument with the Lord, because I am only saying exactly what He said.

Lukewarmness! This church said, "We are rich; we have gotten riches; we have need of nothing." Do you feel like that? Oh, we love these conferences. We are rich; we have gotten riches. We have need of nothing; we feel so sorry for those poor people in such and such a denomination, and those others in that denomination. But we are really something. We've got it; we've seen.

Note the threatened action: "I am coming to you and will remove your lampstand out of its place." "I will spew you out of My mouth."

We often take Revelation 3:20 as being an evangelistic message: "Behold, I stand at the door and knock: if any man hear my voice and open the door, I will come in to him, and will sup with him, and he with me."

I myself found the Lord on that verse, so I am very thankful for it, but it is not an evangelistic message in the first place. It is to a New Testament church, a real church that the Lord had been cold-shouldered out of by lukewarmness; not by outright frigidity, not by outright antagonism; just lukewarmness. He was outside, knocking: "Behold, I stand at the door of the church here, of the living church of the house of God, and I knock. Is there any one who can hear Me? If any man hears My voice and opens the door, I will come in and will sup with Him and He with Me." It is the renewal of love.

There can be no genuine fulfillment of God's purpose, no reaching of His goal without love. That is the message of the book of Revelation. All those other wonderful visions and mysteries, we will leave to another time. But the message that runs right through it, more essential than any of the others is this: If you do not keep within your first love, you will never come to the throne. You will never reach God's goal. You will never be part of that bride of His.

The Essential Nature of First Love

I want to say something about the essential nature of first love to explode any false ideas. First love is a quality of love. It is not an indication of its sequence in time. Most people think of first love (may I use a colloquial slang) as puppy love. So we think: Oh, the Lord says you have left your first affection, your first explosion of emotion, you have left your "puppy love," when you were all doe-eyed and sort of walking on air with Me. That is not what the Lord said at all. First love is not an indication of its sequence in time; it is a quality of love. It is a sensitive love which is totally, completely committed to the object of its love.

What does it mean? It is the kind of love that is ready for any sacrifice, at any time, in any place, for the one it loves.

It will go anywhere, be anything, do anything, spend anything, out of love for that one. First love is ready for a week of prayer, a night of prayer, ready to put aside the routine and wait on God. That is first love. It does not immediately raise a million objections: "Oh, we can't do that; we will upset that, we will upset this. Oh, no, no." First love says, "We will do it." First love will cause a person to fall into the ground and die in a place like New Guinea or somewhere in the Amazon or in some industrial dark area of a North American city. Such is first love.

I cannot tell you how moved I was some years ago when I was taken by an old and godly servant of the Lord, to a little unknown place in the mountains of Benjamin north of Jerusalem. (This sister had served the Lord with Rees Howells and others for many years, and then in the latter part of her life served in Israel.) There I met three aged Moravian sisters. The leader of them was eighty-four years of age. I had not for many, many years touched the Lord in a person as I did in her.

On the day that I went, which was quite some time ago, these sisters had spent the whole day washing the clothes of the thirteen lepers that were their charge. The Arab women and men who came in would not touch the clothes, so these sisters did it instead. Day in, day out, for forty-two years that Moravian sister had cared for lepers. One of them had no legs, no arms, blind in one eye, another one had no feet and only one hand and no nose. They had to be carried to the bathroom, they had to be fed, washed, and everything done for them.

No one knows of these sisters. No one has sung about them. No one has written about them. They are not popular. They have never been thanked. They come from a mother house in Eastern

Germany from which they are cut off, so even their money is very little. I was more humbled by my visit to them than by many, many other visits I have paid to other servants of the Lord.

I only mention this because I saw in that sister a first love. She never said, "Oh, this terrible work, get people to pray for us." She was radiant. When the sister who had taken me there said to me, "They have been washing the clothes of the lepers all day," I couldn't believe it. They were radiant, full of the Spirit of the Lord. They were three seeds that had fallen into the ground and died. I cannot help feeling that such must come to the throne. Somewhere, sometime there must be some recognition. That is first love. There was no thought of being popular, of being written about, of being famous. At least if you lay down your life, it is nice to know that people know it and sort of say, "Wasn't it wonderful? So and so laid down his life. Did you see it?" But to do it where no one sees you, when no one knows really, and perhaps, it seems nobody cares—that is first love.

First love is a quality that God looks for in you and me. Think of 1 Corinthians 13. Many of you have got that up on the wall, written on some plaque or parchment on the wall because it is so wonderful. But I wonder if anyone has ever noticed the searing nature of the words.

"If I speak with the tongues of men and angels, but have not love, I am become sounding brass, or a clanging cymbal. And if I have the gift of prophecy, and know all mysteries and all knowledge; and if I have all faith, so as to remove mountains, but have not love, I am nothing. And if I bestow all my goods to feed the poor, and if I give my body to be burned, but have not love, it profiteth me nothing" (1 Corinthians 13:1–3).

Forget the sentiment for a moment. These words are searing. "If I had the tongues of men and angels (many would so desire), but have not love, I am become sounding brass." "A noisy gong" is how the New American Standard Bible puts it. I wonder how many noisy gongs there are here, how many clanging cymbals?

Or again, listen to this: "If I have the gift of prophecy and know *all* mysteries and *all* knowledge and have not love, I am nothing"—a noisy gong, a clanging cymbal, nothing. "And if I bestow *all* my goods to feed the poor and if I give my body to be burned, but have not love, it profits me nothing." First love. What an indictment! Years of work, of zeal, of study, of energy, even of faith to remove mountains, of sacrifice, even of revelation, and it amounts to nothing.

The Divine Solution

What is the divine solution? God does not give a diagnosis without a solution. Here it is: "Remember from where you have fallen." Did you hear that? "Remember from where you have fallen." Go back and think; Remember. It is the first part of the solution.

Here is the second part. In chapter 2:5 He says, "Repent." Twice He says it. In chapter 3:19 He says: "Be zealous therefore, and repent." Don't think that you cannot repent. When God tells us to repent, every one of us can repent. Some people think you only repent when you get converted. No, God says to believers in the church in Ephesus: "Repent, or else I am coming to you and will remove your lampstand out of its place, except you repent."

What is repentance? It is to turn deliberately toward God and say, "Oh God, forgive me; I repent of this thing. It is not just a failing, a weakness. I cannot make excuses."

We are all people of excuses: "Oh Lord, You know, I am so busy. You know I have so many circumstances. You know the problems with the family. You know the problems with so and so or so and so." But the Lord says, "No, it does not wash. I do not want any excuses. Repent. Be zealous therefore and repent, and do the first works."

What does He mean *the first works*? He means all the things you are doing that are right, only with first love. Maybe you must give your goods; maybe your body will be burned one day. Certainly you should have faith to remove mountains. We have plenty of them that need removing. You ought to have a knowledge of mysteries. Wouldn't it be wonderful if you had a knowledge of all mysteries? I would like to talk with you. I wish you had the tongues of men and angels—with first love. No wonder the apostle says when he ends this marvelous word: "Make love your aim." (Phillips) In another version it says, "Pursue love. This is the most excellent way."

Dear brothers and sisters, it is never easy to talk like this, but we have to at times. Would to God that every one of us was still in our first love but if we are not, may God get through to you and me. May there be tears shed and hearts melted. Somehow or other, may God bring us back into that first love, so that we will not be among those whose love waxes cold because iniquity abounds, but we shall be those who put on the breastplate of faith and love and for a helmet the hope of salvation. The divine diagnosis: "You have left your first love. Repent and do the first works or else I am coming and will remove your lampstand out of its place except you repent."

Shall we pray?

Dear Lord, we pray, in Thy great compassion and mercy and love, do be gracious to us. Thou knowest our hearts altogether, Lord. There is nothing we can hide from Thee. Thou knowest the condition of them. Thou knowest the condition, Lord, of all the companies of Thy children that are represented in this place. Oh Lord, we pray that we may have an ear to hear what Thou art saying and a will to obey Thee and to respond to Thee. Dear Lord, work in our hearts we pray by Your Spirit. We are living in days of great danger and crisis and change. We pray, oh Lord, that we shall be those who by Thy grace are overcomers.

And Lord, we pray if we have left our first love, bring us back, whatever the cost, whatever it means, however much it means we must humble ourselves. If we have to go to one another and confess things, if we have to apologize to one another, if there are things that need to be forgiven and forgotten, cleansed away, give us grace, Lord. We pray that we may have no obstacle in returning to our first love. Help us to understand for each one of us, if this word is applied to us, what "repent" means. When Thou didst say, "Be zealous and repent," help us to understand what it means for us to be zealous and to repent. Lord, have mercy upon us, and by Thy Spirit move in all our hearts we pray. Thou dost love us so much. Win us again to Thyself. We ask it for Thy name's sake. Amen.

4.
The Divine Demonstration

1 John 3:13–16

Marvel not, brethren, if the world hateth you. We know that we have passed out of death into life, because we love the brethren. He that loveth not abideth in death. Whosoever hateth his brother is a murderer: and ye know that no murderer hath eternal life abiding in him. Hereby know we love, because he laid down his life for us: and we ought to lay down our lives for the brethren.

1 John 4:7–21

Beloved, let us love one another: for love is of God; and every one that loveth is begotten of God, and knoweth God. He that loveth not knoweth not God; for God is love. Herein was the love of God manifested in us, that God hath sent his only begotten Son into the world that we might live through him. Herein is love, not that we loved God, but that he loved us, and sent his Son to be the propitiation for our sins. Beloved, if God so loved us, we also ought to love one another. No man hath beheld God at any time: if we love one another, God abideth in us, and his love is perfected in us: hereby we know that we abide in him and he in us, because he hath given us of his Spirit. And we have beheld and bear witness that the Father hath sent the Son to be the Saviour of the world. Whosoever shall confess that Jesus is the Son of God, God abideth in him, and he in God. And we know and have believed the love which God hath in us. God is love; and he that abideth in love abideth in God, and God abideth in him. Herein is love made perfect with us, that we may have boldness in the day of judgment; because as he is, even so are we in this world. There is no fear in love: but perfect love casteth out fear, because fear hath punishment; and he that feareth is not made perfect in love. We love, because he first loved us. If a man say, I love God, and hateth his brother, he is a liar: for he that loveth not his brother whom he hath seen, cannot love God whom he hath not seen. And this commandment have we from him, that he who loveth God love his brother also.

Shall we bow in a word of prayer?

Oh heavenly Father, we are so thankful that this evening hast not taken Thee by surprise, and we are glad therefore that Thou hast made a special provision of grace and power for this time. Now Lord, we take that grace and power. We pray for the one who speaks that Thou wilt give him strength in voice and that Thou wilt help all of us to hear physically the words, as well as to hear what Thou art seeking to say through the human language. Oh Father, how glad we are that Thou hast given us an anointing, and by faith, together, we stand into that anointing that it may operate fully in this time. In spite of all these difficult conditions may we be enabled to overcome and to meet with Thee and to receive from Thee and hear Thy voice. And we ask this together in the name of our Lord Jesus. Amen.

I have had this burden about the love of God based on that little verse in Philippians 1:9: "And this I pray, that your love may abound yet more and more in knowledge and all discernment; that ye may approve the things that are excellent; that ye may be sincere and void of offence unto the day of Christ."

I want to speak on what I have entitled "The Divine Demonstration." God has demonstrated His love in a supreme way. Of course, everything about God is a demonstration of love. Bethlehem is a demonstration of love. The ministry of the Lord Jesus Christ for those three years or more was a demonstration of love. But it was His work on Calvary that was the supreme demonstration of love. We read in Revelation 1:5–6: "Unto him that loveth us, and loosed us from our sins by his blood; and he made us to be a kingdom, to be priests unto his God and Father; to him be the glory and the dominion for ever and ever."

What wonderful words! Or again that very well known verse known to everyone: "For God so loved the world, that He gave His only begotten Son, that whosoever believeth on Him should not perish, but have everlasting life" (John 3:16).

In 1 John 3:16 we see the demonstration of His love: "Hereby know we love, because he laid down his life for us."

Or again: "Herein was the love of God manifested in us, that God hath sent his only begotten Son into the world that we might live through him. Herein is love, not that we loved God, but that he loved us, and sent his Son to be the propitiation for our sins...We love, because he first loved us" (1 John 4:9–10, 19).

The Mystery of the Cross

I would like you for a few moments to consider the mystery of the cross. In all the mysteries that there are in the Bible, there is no mystery as fathomless, as immeasurable, as incomprehensible as the mystery of the cross. It was six short hours, from 9:00 in the morning till 3:00 in the afternoon, that Jesus, the Messiah, finished the work of our salvation and saved to the uttermost everyone who comes to God by Him—six hours on one day, in time. We can fall very easily into a trap of thinking, a way of thought, that somehow because it was only six hours of suffering it must have been easy for the Lord Jesus, relatively speaking. It must have been a light burden for Him, relatively speaking. It could not have cost Him so much—six hours. Many of us have known people personally who have suffered, not for six hours physically and mentally, but for months and months and some of them for years. There are martyrs who have suffered far, far more than six hours. What then really happened on the cross?

Sometimes, because our salvation is the free gift of God—we pay nothing, we can do nothing, it is given to us by God freely and of grace—we imagine that it is cheap. Because it costs us nothing in one sense except unpopularity and a humbling of ourselves before God and before men, we think that this salvation was cheap. But into those few hours of time was condensed a suffering, a world of anguish, of death that is beyond comprehension and beyond computation. It was a world of suffering and of death contracted into a few hours in the person of the Messiah. It was a measureless cost. It was a fathomless pain. It is far beyond all human comprehension. Neither the greatest theological minds in the world nor the most devout spirits who have ever been saved by the grace of God can fully comprehend what it cost the Lord Jesus to save us. It is beyond human computation. Only God the Father and God the Spirit know what the Son did on the cross and the price that He paid. It is essential mystery that we face.

How did Christ become sin for us? In the inspired words of the apostle Paul, how was He who knew no sin made our sin, that we might become the righteousness of God in Him? Can anyone explain it? To what extent did He become our sin? What did the Father do to Him? Human language, even when divinely inspired, is totally inadequate to describe or define exactly what happened in those six hours on the cross.

Indeed, it is a noteworthy fact that none of the evangelists try to tell us exactly what happened. All they do is describe the outward facts in an almost journalistic style. They say, "At 9:00 o'clock He was nailed to the cross and He prayed, 'Father, forgive them, they know not what they do.'" Then they just tell us the different things that happened—the cries, the torments, the jeers, the darkness that came, the final great cry of the Lord Jesus Christ. They tell us that the veil was rent in two. It is almost journalistic. They do not try to define exactly what happened in those six hours. And they certainly do not explain how He became sin for us. I think that is a noteworthy fact.

Furthermore, there is another noteworthy fact. The evangelists do not dwell upon the physical sufferings of the Lord Jesus. Sometimes Christians make a great mistake by somehow trying to describe all the different aspects of crucifixion. Now crucifixion is a hideous and horrific death. But it is a most interesting thing that none of the evangelists, nor any of the writers of the letters of the New Testament dwell upon the physical sufferings of Christ. It is as if they are saying to us: "Those physical sufferings, the outward cries, the outward acts are the least part of this story. The real story is unknowable, untellable. It is in the invisible; it is what happens behind what is seen. So they do not even try to tell us.

It is an interesting fact that nowhere do the apostles and other writers of the rest of the New Testament try to tell us in detail how Jesus bore away the sin of the world, or how He became the sin of the world, or what tasting death for every man actually meant. They do not try to describe it, or define it, or fully explain it. They just tell us the facts in the most glorious manner. They say, "He died, the Just for the unjust that He might bring us to God." They say, "He that knew no sin was made sin for us that we might become the righteousness of God in Him." They simply tell us the facts and the glorious consequences of which they were witnesses and of which they had real and original experience.

All this I find of tremendous import. In fact, if I may say it, it is a most remarkable fact that the greatest, most detailed account of what happened to Jesus in those six hours on the cross is not found anywhere in the New Testament; it is found in the Old Testament in Psalm 22. In the four gospels you have the eye witness accounts of spectators watching the form of the Messiah on the cross suffering and dying. But in Psalm 22 you have the whole scene described, not by a spectator watching the person die and suffer in the midst, but through the eyes of the One who was pierced in His hands and His feet. It is a most remarkable account for that very reason.

Furthermore, if we believe in the tradition, King David authored Psalm 22. Yet while we have the history of King David chronicled, nowhere can we find him having any such experience as having his hands and his feet being pierced, or people gathering around him and jeering, and so on. It is an amazing account.

Furthermore, nowhere in the New Testament do we have a more detailed definition of what the Messiah did in those six hours than in Isaiah 53. That goes farther than anything you will find, even in the New Testament, in describing how He was wounded for our transgressions, how He was bruised for our iniquities, how the chastisement of our peace fell upon Him, and how with His stripes we are healed.

There are some people who perhaps feel subconsciously (though they would not say it outwardly) that since Jesus was God surely it was relatively easy for Him to save us on the cross, as if what He did on the cross was a kind of sham. He went through something in order to satisfy the legal requirements of our being justified, and saved, and delivered. This is a lie.

In Mark 15:33 we read this: "And when the sixth hour was come, there was darkness over the whole land until the ninth hour." From noon until three o'clock in the afternoon, a darkness came over the whole land. The very light of the sun faded. Now those of you who know a few things about the universe will know that this could not have been an eclipse. Some people tell us that it was an eclipse of the sun, but there has never been and could never be an eclipse of the sun for three hours.

What then happened when the light of the sun failed and darkness came over the whole earth unless the answer is found in a little verse in Colossians 1:17? It says, "In him all things hold together." And when Jesus was made sin for us, it was as if a sword went not only through the heart of the creation but through the very Godhead. It was as if God (may I speak without blaspheming) shuddered, halted, hesitated for a moment, contracted within Himself, as if the universe trembled and the natural light and energy of the universe faded for three hours.

Dear friends, for me that speaks volumes. It means that this six hours on the cross was no cheap, easy matter but in some way it cost God everything to save us. The real story of what happened on the cross in those six hours is unknowable and untellable. The real price that He paid, how He was made sin for us, we shall never really know. The outward facts that have been recorded for us are the merest indication of that unseen and untellable story. It is as if we stand on the brink of an ocean of unutterable, inexplicable, incommunicable anguish, and all we can do is bow our heads in worship because here we have the demonstration of love such as this world has never, ever known. This is the mystery of the cross.

I do not think any child of God will ever be delivered from cheapness, from familiarity, from not fearing the Lord, until they come face to face with the mystery of the cross. Sometimes the way we behave, sometimes the way we speak almost sounds as if it were the easiest thing in the world for God to save us. But it was not. Love paid a price that not a single one of the saints would ever be able to comprehend individually, nor all of us put together.

The Work of the Cross

I would like to say something about the work of the cross. What happened? As I have said, we shall never fully know but at least there are some Scriptures that bring us face to face with this mystery and the glory of it. We will just go through these Scriptures, and maybe they will leave you with an understanding, at least of the love of God for you and for me, such as you have not had before.

II Corinthians 5:21: "Him who knew no sin God made to be sin for us; that we might become the righteousness of God in him."

Did you hear these well-known words? Him who knew no sin—the sinless one, God made to be sin for us; that we might be made the righteousness of God, God's righteousness in Him. It is a divine exchange. He was made my sin and I have been made His righteousness. Can anyone explain it? Can anyone understand it?

Isaiah 53:6: "All we like sheep have gone astray; we have turned every one to his own way; and the Lord hath laid on him the iniquity of us all." In the Hebrew the word "And the Lord hath laid on him the iniquity of us all" is this: "And the Lord has caused to gather on Him, to meet in Him the iniquity of us all." This word "iniquity" is the strongest word in the Bible for sin. All the iniquity of the world from Adam to the last one that will ever live was caused to gather on Him, to meet in Him. The iniquity of Adolph Hitler, the iniquity of Mussolini, the iniquity of Stalin, the iniquity of Nero, the iniquity of all these evil, demonized men, and your iniquity and my iniquity, the iniquity of every century of time, all of it was caused to gather in Him, to meet in Him. "All we like sheep have gone astray. We have turned every one to his own way and the Lord has laid on Him the iniquity of us all."

John 1:29: "Behold, the Lamb of God, that taketh away the sin of the world!" The lamb is one of the sweetest creatures in the world. A little lamb, by its very being, is a symbol of purity, of life, of freshness, of almost sinlessness, of spring. "Behold, the Lamb of God who beareth away the sin of the world."

John 3:14: "And as Moses lifted up the serpent in the wilderness, even so must the Son of man be lifted up; that whosoever believeth may in him have eternal life." Did you hear that? "As Moses lifted up the serpent in the wilderness, even so must the Son of Man be lifted up." How has the Lamb become the lifted-up serpent? What has happened that somehow the Lamb should have become a lifted-up serpent? Why a serpent? I think the serpent is the exact opposite of everything the lamb is. It is cunning, full of guile, full of poison, somehow, as it were, related to death, to darkness. It belongs to an underworld almost. How is it that that poison which has come into the blood stream of humanity, of mankind, has been put upon the Lamb? And the Lamb in some way has become the up-lifted serpent, so that all of us, bitten by this evil, by this power of darkness, by God's great adversary, can have eternal life in Him.

Galatians 3:13: "Christ redeemed us from the curse of the law, having become a curse for us; for it is written, Cursed is every one that hangeth on a tree."

This word "cursed" in the Hebrew means excommunicated, banned, put outside of the covenant people, thrown out of the redeemed community. That is how it was looked upon. And Jesus became a curse for us. He was made sin for us. All our iniquity was laid on Him. The Lamb of God which takes away the sin of the world became the up-lifted serpent so that anyone who looks to Him may in Him have eternal life. We who were under the curse and already excommunicated may be reconciled to God.

Mark 14:27: "And Jesus saith unto them, All ye shall be offended: for it is written, I will smite the shepherd, and the sheep shall be scattered abroad." Jesus was quoting from the prophet Zechariah, but the prophet Zechariah did not quite put it that way. This is how he put it in the Hebrew version in Zechariah 13:7: "Awake, O sword, against my shepherd, and against the man that is my fellow, saith the Lord." Now the Septuagint says exactly the same. So it is to me an inescapable conclusion that the Lord Jesus made it abundantly clear when He quoted the prophet Zechariah that when God said "Awake, O sword, against my shepherd, against the man who is my fellow, saith the Lord," that it was the Lord who was smiting Him. He said, "It is written, I will smite the shepherd, and the sheep shall be scattered."

So now we at least understand that the Lord Jesus in those six hours was made sin for us, and when the Lamb of God who taketh away the sin of the world became the up-lifted serpent, God struck Him. And in that moment, out of His anguished heart was torn the cry recorded in Mark 15:34: "My God, my God, why hast thou forsaken me?" That was the moment when darkness came over the face of the earth, when somehow God withdrew from His Son, and when the Lord Jesus, being made sin for us, was struck by God.

Hebrews 2:9: "But we behold him who hath been made a little lower than the angels, even Jesus, because of the suffering of death crowned with glory and honor, that by the grace of God he should taste of death for every man."

A vast universe of sin, a vast world of iniquity, a world of abomination was all placed upon Him and done away with. He tasted all the pain of history, all the sickness and disease of history, all the death that is our common lot, and it was all condensed into the experience of six hours. And in that work which He finished, He took with Him into death an old world order, an old creation poisoned by the serpent, a man, an old man, an old nature who could never satisfy God and never serve God acceptably.

At the end of those six hours, Jesus cried in weakness, "I thirst." He was given vinegar to drink, a kind of sour wine, and then suddenly, He shouted with a loud voice. And John the apostle says, "He cried, 'Finished!'" In that moment the veil of the temple, with those great cherubim woven on it, was torn in two from top to bottom. The Talmud tells us it was enormous—seven, eight hands thick. What a shock for the priest on duty that day when suddenly he heard the sound of a mighty wind, a rushing noise like a great steam engine going through the sanctuary, and looking round he saw what must have seemed to him blasphemy. The veil in the temple was torn from top to bottom and he stood gazing into the Holiest of Holies. It is no wonder to me that the Acts of the apostles said that a great company of the priests and Levites believed. The story must have gone right through them all, what with the earthquake, and the saints who rose from their tombs and appeared to people in the city. They must have thought:

What is it? It happened exactly the moment He died, the moment He cried. That moment it happened.

John's Revelation of the Lamb Slain

Dear people of God, I have no doubt that the enemy would do anything to stop us from really understanding even a little of the mystery of the cross. Some people think this is kindergarten stuff. That shows how trite and stupid they are. This is not kindergarten stuff; this lies at the very heart of the kingdom of God. For when John the apostle, looking into eternity, saw the rainbow-encircled throne of God and saw the One who was and who is and who is to come sitting on the throne, He saw in His hand the scroll with seven seals, sealed up. Any Jew knew that was a testament, a will, an inheritance. And when the voice said, "Who can break the seals? Who can fulfill the purpose of God? Who can secure for God what He has ever desired?" no one moved in heaven or on earth or under the earth. And John burst into tears. Then an angel came and touched him and said, "John, don't cry, look!" And John turned toward the throne and there in the midst of the throne of Him who was and who is and who is to come, the eternal, He saw a little lamb as it had been slain, standing, having seven horns, and seven eyes, which are the seven Spirits of God. And He took the scroll out of His hand and He broke first one seal, and then the next, and the next, and the next, and the next, until the seven seals were broken. Then all kinds of things began to happen as John watched. He saw vision after vision after vision. And out of the seven seals came seven trumpets, and out of the seven trumpets came seven bowls, and at the end of the seventh bowl Babylon was destroyed. Then there was a great hallelujah that went up from the whole assembled multitude in heaven: "Hallelujah: for the Lord our God, the Almighty reigns. Let us rejoice and be exceeding glad, for the marriage supper of the Lamb is come, and his wife has made herself ready."

Dear, dear people of God, I can never tell you how much I am humbled before God, and I am sure you must feel the same, to believe that He loved you and that He loved me so much that He gave Himself to save us. He saved us to bring us into this purpose of love, to bring us into this bride of love, to bring us into this city of glory, to bring us into this eternal vocation. It is a love story from beginning to end. Has anyone, even those dearest and nearest to you, ever put on you the price that the Lord Jesus placed on you? Has anyone ever put a cost on saving you and delivering you that God has put on you? How wonderful all this is when you really think about this demonstration of God's love.

Some people say to me: "How do I know God loves me?" Oh, that the Spirit of God would touch the eyes of their hearts! Here is the supreme demonstration of the love of God. We love because He first loved us. When we were ugly, when we were dead in sins, when we were blind in our willfulness, when we hated Him or ignored Him, He had us in mind and He gave Himself for us. I can think of no more wonderful word than the word of the apostle Paul: "He loved me and gave Himself for me."

The Result of God's Great Love

What is the result of all this? The result it seems to me can only be what we find in Romans 8:31–39: What then shall we say to these things? If God is for us, who is against us? He that spared not his own Son, but delivered him up for us all, how shall he not also with him freely give us all things? Who shall lay anything to the charge of God's elect? It is God that justifieth; who is he that condemneth? It is Christ Jesus that died, yea rather, that was raised from the dead, who is at the right hand of God, who also maketh intercession for us. Who shall separate us from the love of Christ? Shall tribulation, or anguish, or persecution, or famine, or nakedness, or peril, or sword? Even as it is written, For thy sake we are killed all the day long; We were accounted as sheep for the slaughter. Nay, in all these things we are more than conquerors through him that loved us. For I am persuaded, that neither death, nor life, nor angels, nor principalities, nor things present, nor things to come, nor powers, nor height, nor depth, nor any other creature, shall be able to separate us from the love of God, which is in Christ Jesus our Lord.

I don't know whether what I have said has somehow awakened a chord in you or met some need in you or given you some little understanding of just how much God loves you. There is a little phrase in the letter of Paul to the Ephesians that says this: "But God, for his great love wherewith he loved us, quickened us together with Christ and raised us up with Him, and made us to set together with Him in heavenly places."

Oh dear child of God, will we ever, ever fathom the love of God? Will we ever be able to walk out of the love of God? Does the love of God have boundaries to which we can come, having somehow exhausted it? No, it is limitless, unsearchable, fathomless, measureless. Oh, what a wonderful thing it is to be loved by God!

Now if this is true, then listen again to the apostle Paul: "I pray that your love may abound yet more and more in knowledge and all discernment; that ye may approve the things which are excellent; that ye may be sincere and void of offence unto the day of Jesus Christ."

Can you understand the apostle Paul's concern? And I believe God has put this burden on me for this very reason. We are moving into times of unparalleled disorder, and change, and shaking, and strife, and darkness. If there is one thing more basic, more essential, more vital than anything else, it is the love of God shed abroad in our hearts. Without it, we are nothing. Without it, everything we do profits us nothing. We are noisy gongs and clanging cymbals. But if we have that quality of first love in us, if that flame of His love engulfs us, then we shall be kept by the power of God in these days that lie ahead. We shall know what it is for the body to build up itself in love. We shall know what it is to be servants one to another through love. We shall know what it is to persevere together until God brings that top stone into its place with shouts of "grace, grace unto it."

The Response to God's Love

Dear people of God, we ought to lay down our lives for the brethren. That is what the apostle John said in 1 John 3:16. I always think it is interesting that John's gospel 3:16 says, "For God so loved the world, that He gave His only begotten Son, that whosoever believeth on him should not perish, but have everlasting life." But in 1 John 3:16 we have the next step: "Hereby know we love, because he laid down his life for us: and we ought to lay down our lives for the brethren." Again in 1 John 4:11: "Beloved, if God so loved us, we also ought to love one another."

I believe this matter of love is not just a luxury or some sentimental ecstasy but is the essential constituent in the things of God? This divine love lies behind the perseverance of God with us. It lies behind the redemption of God. It lies behind the atoning work of the Lord Jesus. It lies behind the gift of the Holy Spirit. It lies behind the sanctifying grace of God. It lies behind the goal of God, the aim of God. Dear people of God, we need this love more than I can ever say. May God inflame your hearts with a hunger and a thirst for Him. May these words come back again and again and again to you. And may He be enabled to find in you and me that response of love, which alone will finally and fully satisfy Him.

There is a beautiful hymn of Charles Wesley, which through the years has been one of my favorites.

O Thou who camest from above
The pure celestial fire to impart,
Kindle a flame of sacred love
On the mean altar of my heart.

There let it for Thy glory burn
With inextinguishable blaze;
And trembling to its source return,
In humble prayer and fervent praise.
Jesus, confirm my heart's desire
To work, and speak, and think for Thee;
Still let me guard the holy fire,

And still stir up Thy gift in me.
Ready for all Thy perfect will,
My acts of faith and love repeat,
Till death Thy endless mercies seal,
And make the sacrifice complete.

Shall we pray?

Oh Lord, when we consider something of the mystery of that finished work of our Lord Jesus on the cross at Golgotha, we are humbled to the dust. Oh forgive us in this twentieth century, Lord, for our lukewarmness, for all our apathy, our indifference, our familiarity with Thy things. We treat this matter of the cross as if it is a thing. We treat our salvation, Lord, as if was somehow easy for Thee because it was free for us. Oh God, give us a glimpse of the measureless cost that Thou didst pay to save us that will change our lives. As that dawns upon our hearts, may a new love be born in us. May that great love of Thine and our little appreciation of it fill us anew and beget in us a love for Thee that will be first love in its quality. And may that love mean that we shall love our neighbor as ourselves. Oh Lord, do this we pray in us. Kindle a sacred flame of love on the mean altar of my heart. Oh God, may we be people in whom the fire of God, the fire of Thy love is found burning yet more and more. And Lord, may we be assemblies, communities, companies of believers all over the world, burning with the love of God, in whom the flame of divine love is found, first love, Lord. Oh God, only Thou canst do this. Baptize us afresh with that love of Thine and grant, oh Lord, that we shall never be the same again. And we ask it together in the name of our Lord Jesus. Amen.

5.
The Divine Method

John 17:12–26

While I was with them, I kept them in thy name which thou hast given me: and I guarded them, and not one of them perished, but the son of perdition; that the scripture might be fulfilled. But now I come to thee; and these things I speak in the world, that they may have my joy made full in themselves. I have given them thy word; and the world hated them, because they are not of the world, even as I am not of the world. I pray not that thou shouldest take them from the world, but that thou shouldest keep them from the evil one. They are not of the world, even as I am not of the world. Sanctify them in the truth: thy word is truth. As thou didst send me into the world, even so sent I them into the world. And for their sakes I sanctify myself, that they themselves also may be sanctified in truth. Neither

---

for these only do I pray, but for them also that believe on me through their word; that they may all be one; even as thou, Father, art in me, and I in thee, that they also may be in us: that the world may believe that thou didst send me. And the glory which thou hast given me I have given unto them; that they may be one, even as we are one; I in them, and thou in me, that they may be perfected into one; that the world may know that thou didst send me, and lovedst them, even as thou lovedst me. Father, I desire that they also whom thou hast given me be with me where I am, that they may behold my glory, which thou hast given me: for thou lovedst me before the foundation of the world. O righteous Father, the world knew thee not, but I knew thee; and these knew that thou didst send me; and I made known unto them thy name, and will make it known; that the love wherewith thou lovedst me may be in them, and I in them.

Shall we pray?

Lord, we pray that as we turn now to Thy word, Thou would be gracious to us and grant we pray that every one of us may receive something from Thyself. We thank Thee, Lord, that Thou has made a special grace and a special power available for this time, and we stand by faith into that provision. We appropriate it in the name of our Lord Jesus, and we look to Thee that both speaker and hearer alike may know that anointing upon them so that together we may fulfill Thy will, may meet with Thee, may receive of Thee. Oh Lord, hear us we pray as we commit ourselves to Thee in the name of our Lord Jesus. Amen.

I have entitled this final word about the love of God "The Divine Method." We are rather afraid of methods but I have called it the divine method or, if you like, the divine way. What a wonderful way the Lord Jesus ended that great prayer of intercession recorded in John 17, that prayer we call the high priestly prayer: "That the love wherewith thou lovedst me may be in them and I in them." Oh, how the Father loves the Son. He did not say, "That the love wherewith thou lovedst me may be shown to them." No. That was so, but He said "may be in them and I in them."

You will remember that it was a sentence in one of the letters of the apostle Paul that started us off on this consideration of the love of God: "And this I pray, that your love may abound yet more and more in knowledge and all discernment; so that ye may approve the things that are excellent; that ye may be sincere and void of offence unto the day of Christ" (Philippians 1:9). We are nearer to that day than ever before in this age. We do not know just how near we are, whether we still have some years to go, a decade or two to go, or whether the day of Jesus Christ might dawn today.

The great prayer of the apostle Paul for that beloved church at Philippi and I suppose for all the churches that were in his care and all the churches that were beyond his province of authority was: "I pray for you that your love may abound yet more and more." Nothing else will keep us in the will of God. Nothing else will enable us to triumph in adversity. Nothing else will enable us to endure all the pressures and strains of the last phase of the end time. Nothing else will enable us to overcome but that love of God in us and the Lord Jesus in us. That is what you and I need more than anything else. That may be why the Lord Jesus ended His great prayer of intercession with these words: "That the love wherewith thou lovedst me may be in them and I in them." If the same love that the Father has for the Son, that same fulness of love, that same power of love be in us, and the Lord Jesus be in us, we must surely be invincible. By the grace of God we shall overcome and stand before His face. We shall come by the grace of God to the throne of God. For nothing else will ever satisfy the Father or the Son or the Spirit other than a heart and a life that is filled, immersed in the love of God.

Bearing Fruit

Even as the Father hath loved me, I also have loved you: abide ye in my love. If ye keep my commandments, ye shall abide in my love; even as I have kept my Father's commandments, and abide in his love. These things have I spoken unto you, that my joy may be in you, and that your joy may be made full. This is my commandment, that ye love one another, even as I have loved you. Greater love hath no man than this, that a man lay down his life for his friends. Ye are my friends, if ye do the things which I command you. No longer do I call you servants; for the servant knoweth not what his lord doeth: but I have called you friends; for all things that I heard from my Father I have made known unto you. Ye did not choose me, but I chose you, and appointed you, that ye should go and bear fruit, and that your fruit should abide: that whatsoever ye shall ask of the Father in my name, he may give it you. These things I command you, that ye may love one another. (John 15:9–17)

What is the divine method? Will you first note here that the Lord's end for us, in one sense, is that we should bear much fruit and that our fruit should remain. It is not transient fruit, not decaying fruit, but fruit that is eternal. "Ye did not choose me, but I chose you, and appointed you, that ye should go and bear much fruit, and that your fruit should remain."

The Jewish people were judged and dispersed to the ends of the earth because there was no fruit. God is always looking for fruit. To be given salvation, to be given revelation, to be given eternal life is a grave responsibility viewed from one aspect because the end must always be fruit. And if we are barren, if we are fruitless, something is wrong.

There are many, many believers that are barren. Indeed, I think one has to say honestly before God that the great majority of us believers are fruitless. We are barren. If we do bring the blossom and the beginning of fruit, it is cast before it comes to ripening. Something goes wrong. It is as if the tree cannot take the fruit. It has the early promise of fruit. There are many people who have real experiences of the Lord, real experiences of the Holy Spirit. You can see the blossom and the beginning of the fruit forming. Then you come a little later and the whole thing has dropped. It is just leaves. There is no fruit; it is all leaves.

It is so with many assemblies of God's people, many companies of God's children. Sometimes you go and you see a real moving of God. God speaks to them; God gives them revelation; God challenges them; there is a real influence, as it were, brought to bear upon them from the throne. It seems as if for awhile they are going to bear fruit. There is a blossom; there is the beginning of fruit forming in the tree. Then you go back, perhaps months later, or a year or two later, and it is all gone. The leaves are there, the life is there, but there is no fruit. But if the Lord Jesus chooses you and appoints you, and sends you to go anywhere, even to the most uncongenial place on earth, you should bear fruit and your fruit should remain.

Laying down Your Life

What then is the key, if it is not this matter of divine love? What if, in all the revelation and all the zeal, the love of God is somehow missing? The Lord Jesus put His finger on this matter infallibly when He said, "Greater love has no man than this that a man lay down his life for his friends." In other words, it was as if the Lord Jesus was saying, "Now look here, it is no good just talking about love, singing about love, praying about love. Love is expressed in action; love is expressed in a way of life; love is expressed in lives laid down. "Greater love hath no man than this that a man lay down his life for his friends."

Why do we not see people saved in the office or in our places of work? Why do we not sometimes see people saved in our families? Why do we not see sometimes people saved in our circle of friends? It is because we give the impression that we know it all, that *we* are the saved, that *we* are something, that *we've* got everything and you should listen because you are going to hell. You are under the wrath of God, you are under the curse. They do not see a life laid down. They do not see all the little jobs done for them out of love. They do not see a deep, real concern. They only see themselves as a head to be counted, as a trophy to be won, as another name to be added to someone's popularity and glory as an evangelist or a teacher or a servant of the Lord or a witness to Jesus Christ. The people are not loved. "Greater love hath no man than this."

Most of us have made these mistakes in our families. When we were first saved, we went back like a steam train, like an express, like Concorde, zooming in with great noise: "Now listen, you, I have been saved." We are full of it. It is not that we are doing anything necessarily wrong, but we have failed to see that the thing that wins a family or wins friends is a character. We have failed to see that by opting out of family responsibilities because we have been saved, we have damaged the reputation of the Lord. By never being the one in the office or in that place of work who bears the burden and cares for people, who loves the people, we have opted out of our responsibility. We have damaged the reputation and the name of the Lord.

"Greater love hath no man than this that a man lay down his life for his friends." Here is the divine method. You cannot lay down your life unless you are filled with love. Try it; try it! All it is, is a dead teaching which brings you into a cast iron bondage. I know many people who talk about the cross all day long and nearly all night long. It goes round and round and round in their head like a spinning top, and what is the result? They look dark, they are dark, they are heavy, they are dour, they are lifeless. They have a kind of self-imposed brokenness. It is not the Lord. When God comes in with a work of the cross, the result is resurrection. And resurrection swallows up the brokenness, so that in you it is death, but it is life in them. You touch the brokenness, the death, the affliction; they touch life, they touch the Lord, they touch the power of God, they touch the glory of God.

"Greater love hath no man than this that he lay down his life for his friends. Ye are my friends." The Lord Jesus does not demand of us anything that He has not done. That is why I spoke before about the divine demonstration. If you and I are not baptized in the love of God, if we are not immersed in the love of God, if the love of God is not being shed abroad in our hearts by the Holy Spirit, if the love of God is not the dynamic of our living, of our service, of our church life, of our worship, then it seems to me that we come only into a formalism. We cannot but come into a formalism. We are barren, we are fruitless. No matter how beautiful or shiny the leaves are or how strong the trunk is, God is not satisfied because He looks for fruit.

In my little ministry of traveling over part of the earth, I go, generally speaking, to those companies of believers that know something about church truth. I don't want to sound condemning or accusing, but I must tell you with a heart that is deeply grieved over much of what I see, that I find again and again that people have church truth but they do not have the church. They have a certain amount of doctrine, a certain amount of vision, a certain amount of understanding, and in spite of the fact that they say again and again it is organic, they try to put it together. It cannot come together without love because the church is a community of love. It is something produced out of the passion of its Lord. When His side was pierced and there came out blood and water, out of that side was brought the bride. Out of that great demonstration, that supreme demonstration of the love of God on Calvary came the church. And if the church contradicts the principle upon which it was born— the love of God—she is nothing. That is why the devil will work and work and work to set us all at sixes and sevens, to spread insinuations and doubts, until we are all suspicious of one another, all disillusioned with one another, all colliding with one another, all, as it were, up against one another, until in the end we cannot win. It is a sham. We take the Lord's Table, it is a sham. We worship, it is a sham. We do not want it to be a sham, but it has become a sham because we have failed to understand that first and greatest commandment: "Thou shalt love the Lord thy God with all thy heart, with all thy soul, with all thy mind, and with all thy strength; and the second greatest commandment: Thou shalt love thy neighbor as thyself."

Church truth is only the beginning of a matter. Thank God if God reveals truth to any brother or sister. There is so much ignorance and so much error in the world that it is a wonderful thing when God reveals anything to any child of God or any servant of God or any company of the Lord's children. But dear ones, remember this, that the understanding of church truth does not automatically bring about the producing of church life. The only thing that brings about the producing of church life is when a few brothers and sisters fall into the ground and die, when they all lay down their lives one for another.

When there is a marriage in which the husband is all "I" and the wife is all "I" and the children are all "I," it is going to be a very unhappy home. Somewhere or other a wife has to lay down her life not only for her children, but for her husband. Somewhere or other a husband has to lay down his life for his wife and for his children. Somewhere or other parents have to lay down their lives for their children. And sometimes there comes a time when children must lay down their lives for their parents. When that happens, you have an atmosphere of love. You have an atmosphere where there is true authority, where there is true order, where there is a real family life, and where it represents something of what God intended. And so it must be with the divine family. You cannot get human beings living together unless they are prepared to lay down their lives for one another and actually do lay down their lives for one another.

The Way of the Cross

If you lay down your life, fruit will be the result. Lay down your life more deeply and there will be more fruit. Lay down your life even more deeply and there will be even more fruit. It is an infallible law with God. So if there is no fruit in your life, whatever your excuse, whatever you say, I can tell you that somewhere the love of God is absent. Somewhere in your life, in my life, the love of God is absent. It is being contradicted, ignored, overlooked. When divine love takes hold of a born again believer, then surely, just as night follows day and day follows night, that believer will be led to the cross. And there in their path, stark and bloody and inescapable is Calvary. For the first time you are faced with whether *you* will fall into the ground and die.

It is not all glory and ecstasy as we sometimes think. We would like a revelation of the cross that would be all ecstatic and full of thrills and lift us up—wonderful, just wonderful. It *is* wonderful when you see that you have been crucified with Christ, but within hours someone will be nailing the nails into your hands. You cannot do it yourself. God has so ordained that your nearest and dearest will do it for you. Within a matter of hours your colleagues, your co-workers, the fellow members of the body of Christ, circumstances, unsaved relatives and friends, your husband, your wife, your children, will be used by God as agents to see that you know what it is to be crucified with Christ. You do not have to bother your head about how to be crucified. The Lord will take care of that; fear not. He has already done it two thousand years ago. But for the application of it in your life, He will use your nearest and dearest, your circumstances, all the people who come into your life to do this very thing in your life. You do not have to worry about it.

We all know that we should lay down our lives, until we come to it. It is all right when it is a lovely feeling that suddenly as we lay down our lives, immediately the Lord will be there to fill us with power and life and joy and revelation. But the Lord often stands back and allows a time where everything is impossible and everything within us screams: "Don't go this way, don't go this way. They will trample over you; they will walk over you; they will destroy you; they will do this and this to you. You will never be the same." Thank God! Haven't you asked the Lord to change you?

"Greater love hath no man than this, that a man lay down his life for his friends." This is the divine method. God has no other method. He has only one method. You must lay down your life. It is the way of the cross.

The Work of the Holy Spirit

Immediately, someone will say, "What about the Holy Spirit?" Quite right, what about the Holy Spirit? The Holy Spirit will only come upon you in fulness and power in an abiding way, not a transient way. Now hear me right on this. There *are* experiences of the Holy Spirit that are transient. There are touches from heaven; there are touches of glory. They come and they go. But there is a coming of the Holy Spirit upon a human being that is forever, not only an indwelling but a committal.

When Jesus came to those waters of Jordan, He did not need to be baptized. He was already righteous; He was without sin. When John the Baptist saw Him, he said, "You should baptize me, not I You." But Jesus said, "Suffer it to be so that righteousness may be fulfilled." What did Jesus mean? He meant something far, far deeper than perhaps most realized, certainly at that time. He meant this: "If I am to do the will of God I have to make a cold-blooded decision today. And that cold-blooded decision is to commit Myself to the death of the cross three years before I come to it." I don't believe anyone helped the Lord Jesus, neither the Father, nor the Spirit. It was a decision that He had to make with His own will as the Son of Man. He chose to go into those waters of Jordan and be baptized. He was really saying, "Father, I love You, and I love this world, and I love those whom You have given to Me out of this world. I commit Myself to the death of the cross that I might win them." In that moment the heavens opened and the Holy Spirit came in a bodily form as a dove and abode upon Him. John said, "I was told that whomever I saw the Holy Spirit coming and abiding upon was the Messiah." He did not just touch

Him, He did not just fill Him and go, He did not just open heaven for a revelation and then close it again. The heavens opened and the Holy Spirit came upon the Lord Jesus and dwelt upon Him.

Many of us have understood the dove as a symbol of meekness, a symbol of gentleness, a symbol of sweetness, and it may be so. But in my estimation that is not the meaning of the Holy Spirit coming down as a dove. John the Baptist knew instantly. He came from a very poor family, and he knew too that Joseph and Mary were poor people. The sacrifice that they made in the temple when they went up three times a year for the great feasts was not a bullock. They could not afford it. Nor was it a lamb; they could not afford it. It was two turtledoves. The moment John the Baptist saw the Holy Spirit coming down in that symbol of sacrifice he said, "Behold the Lamb of God who taketh away the sin of the world." He understood instantly that the Holy Spirit had come upon the Lord Jesus to enable Him to lay down His life that the sin question might be forever settled.

It is not different with you or with me. Only when you will to do the will of God in a cold blooded way and commit yourself to the death of the cross, even though you may not fully understand it, are you a candidate for the Holy Spirit to come upon you and enable you to do what you cannot do yourself. There is no way for you to do it yourself. Try; try to die for other people; try to fall into the ground and die; try to be humble; try to be broken; try to lay down your life for the church and for the world. You cannot do it. You may do it for a day, but believe me you will be exhausted. You will nearly be in a mental home with a nervous breakdown by the end of a month of trying to lay down your life for others. It is impossible. It is unnatural to the fallen nature. It is unnatural to our self-centeredness, to our instinct of self-preservation. Only the Holy Spirit indwelling us and coming upon us can enable us to really lay down our lives so that all that sordid ambition, all that desire for assertion, all that desire to be something, to fight for our rights, or whatever else, is finally dealt with. It is not dealt with in one single moment. It is a lifetime, but the Holy Spirit is there to enable us to do it.

If Jesus, who was without sin, needed the Holy Spirit to die daily for three and a half years of public ministry, how much more do you and I? If Jesus, who was perfect and holy and righteous, needed the Holy Spirit so that He could go through those three and a half years and fulfill His ministry and finally offer Himself up to God without spot or blemish, how much more do you and I need the Holy Spirit to come upon us? It is the divine method.

Maybe you are saying: "Now I see what you are talking about. You are talking about an experience of the Holy Spirit. Ah, I am glad." Others may say, "Oh dear, now what is he up to?" No, please I don't want to say anything that is wrong in the presence of the Holy Spirit but He understands far more than I since He gave me the understanding in the first place. It is not an experience of the Holy Spirit that you need in the first place; it is love. It is only when the love of God has touched your heart, initially perhaps, in a first way that turns you toward the Father, that turns you toward the Lord Jesus, that turns you toward His church, that turns you toward His will, and for the first time you are faced with this possibility: Shall I lay down my life or not?

The Joy of the Lord

In John 15:11 it says, "These things have I spoken unto you, that my joy may be in you, and that your joy may be made full."

One has to say that there are very few Christians that have joy. Isn't it so? We are not talking about that bubbly, effervescent thing, although now and again even that is a relief. But we are not talking about that bubbly, effervescent type of joy that the world knows when it gets hilarious and then commits suicide the same night. It is one of the tragedies of the world because it is a façade. It is not joy. Many Christians have fallen into the same thing. They can come into a meeting where there is a worked up, emotional atmosphere where all is apparently joy, but it isn't. When you get out of it, you fall flat on your face. Taken away from it, you will spiritually die.

What did the Lord Jesus mean when He said, "These things have I spoken unto you, that My joy may be in you"? That is the beginning—His joy. It is not my joy but His joy, and when His joy is in me then my joy is made full. That is the right way round. That is why when we seek to pursue our own satisfaction, and fulness, and fulfillment, we become joyless.

There is only one way for His joy to be in us and that is when we go the way He went. When we go the way He went, His joy is in us and our joy is made full. Don't think for a single moment that when you go the way of the cross it is all dark, all morbid, all dreadful. No, no, no! There is a joy that is made full. God delights to do things for people who have let go. He cooks up the most amazing surprises for them. Sometimes He will leave you for years and years to go through a lonely way of difficulty and problems and then at the end He will come with little surprises that only love could conceive.

There is a wonderful word in the Old Testament that says, "Delight thyself also in the Lord; and he will give thee the desires of thy heart" (Psalm 37:4). I think that is one of the most amazing promises in the word of God. So few people have the desires of their heart. But if you delight yourself in the Lord—and that is more than just obeying, more than just following out of duty, more than just an understanding or a knowing of the will of God—it is a life of worship. It is a life of delight in the Lord, of transport in the Lord. He gives you the desires of your heart.

Friends of God

Another wonderful thing I have found in John 15 is in verse 15. It says, "No longer do I call you servants; for the servant knoweth not what his lord doeth: but I have called you friends; for all things that I heard from my Father I have made known unto you." I think that is a wonderful word. To His friends He divulges His heart. The secret of the Lord is given to us. The Lord does not give His secrets to everybody and He does not divulge His heart to everybody. But if we are prepared to lay down our lives, then there is a kind of revelation, a manifestation of the love of God to us.

The Commandment to Love

"This is my commandment, that ye love one another, even as I have loved you" (John 15:12). There is no other way for the body to be built up in the end, is there? How interesting it is that 1 Corinthians 13 comes in the middle of a passage all to do with church life, with the gifts of the church, with the functions of the body, with the disorders that have to do with the Lord's Table, and all these things. Right in the middle of it, suddenly the apostle says, "Now I will show you a most excellent way." It is as if the Spirit of God said to the apostle: "Don't let them think that it is just a matter of functions and gifts, and exercising these things, and manifesting the Spirit. There is more to it than this.

Then comes 1 Corinthians 13: "If I speak with the tongues of men and angels and have not love, I am a noisy gong and a clanging symbol," and so on. Then he ends that passage by saying, "Pursue love, follow after love," or as Phillips puts it: "Make love your aim."

The Building Up of the Church

In Ephesians 4:16, it speaks of the building up of the body of the Lord and it says, "It maketh the increase of the body unto the building up of itself in love." It is the divine method.

"This is my commandment, that ye love one another, even as I have loved you." How did the Lord love you? He loved you when you were an ugly, impossible, self-centered, self-seeking, empty, hell-deserving sinner. And when you were in that state—blind, dead in sins, darkened in your mind, alienated from God—He loved you. That is how we are to love one another, but we don't. Our brother has only to display one fault and straightway we get all upset. It is strange what the Lord Jesus said about taking the beam out of our own eye before we take the fleck out of our brother's eye. Very often the fleck in our brother's eye is the beam in ours, only we just cannot see it. It is only when God gives us an understanding of ourselves and we take the thing out that we suddenly realize, "I had no right to speak about so and so like that; I have it ten times more."

"Even as I also loved you." Can anybody finish with another believer? If you are disillusioned with another believer, if you are disappointed with another believer, if all you can see in another believer are the failings, the faults, the weaknesses, the frailty, God has not yet done too much in you. Or if He has, pride has come and taken over.

How are you to love your brother? Not because he is perfect, not because he has only one per cent of faults, not because he has only ten per cent of faults. You are to love him as if he has one hundred per cent of faults. That is how the Lord loved you. It is amazing how sometimes the Lord takes five years to get us through an issue, but we get disillusioned with another brother or sister because they have not got through in a week. We say, "They went to that conference and they did not settle it." We forget that it may have taken us ten years before the Lord almost dragged us in and finally met us, and we came through. Then we turn around and say, "Why hasn't it happened to so and so? Something is wrong." Oh, if we could only understand how God has dealt with you and me, then perhaps we would understand a good deal more about one another.

And what helped you most? Was it that someone was standing there like some old school master, grimacing at you with a thunderous brow? Did that help you? Did those people help you who were forever pointing out all your failings and faults?

Did they? Did it help you when someone outlined from Scripture where you were falling so far short and what you ought to be and what you are not? Did it help you? Or was it the person that you felt in your heart had a real, shrewd suspicion of just what you were, but loved you just the same? We all know such people. In our spiritual history there have been people who loved us in spite of what we were; who knew, and yet somehow they were faithful. They spoke the truth in love, but they loved us. Those were the people who built us up. Those were the people who finally brought us to the place where we would break down in tears and melt before God. Those were the ones who helped us on with God. Oh, the damage we do to one another [in] the building up of the church.

Love to the Uttermost

Now before the feast of the passover, Jesus knowing that his hour was come that he should depart out of this world unto the Father, having loved his own that were in the world, he loved them unto the end [loved them to the uttermost]. And during supper, the devil having already put into the heart of Judas Iscariot, Simon's son, to betray him, Jesus, knowing that the Father had given all things into his hands, and that he came forth from God, and goeth unto God, riseth from supper, and layeth aside his garments; and he took a towel, and girded himself. Then he poureth water into the basin, and began to wash the disciples' feet, and to wipe them with the towel wherewith he was girded ... So when he had washed their feet, and taken his garments, and sat down again, he said unto them, Know ye what I have done to You? Ye call me, Teacher, and, Lord: and ye say well; for so I am. If I then, the Lord and the Teacher, have washed your feet, ye also ought to wash one another's feet. For I have given you an example, that ye also should do as I have done to you. Verily, verily, I say unto you, A servant is not greater than his lord; neither one that is sent greater than he that sent him. If ye know these things, blessed are ye if ye do them...A new commandment I give unto you, that ye love one another; even as I have loved you, that ye also love one another. By this shall all men know that ye are my disciples, if ye have love one to another (John 13:1–5, 12–17, 34–35).

What a beautiful phrase this is at the beginning of this marvelous chapter: "Having loved His own who were in the world He loved them to the uttermost." I like that much more than "to the end." It was not that there was an end of the Lord's love or a point of time when He finished. He loved them to the uttermost. Jesus, the Messiah, Jesus, the Son of Man, Jesus, in whom all the fulness of the Father dwells in bodily form, Jesus, God the Son, took a towel, laid aside His outer garment, girded Himself with the towel, took a basin and filled it with water. Then He knelt in front of each of His disciples and washed their feet. It is almost too much for the mind. Can God kneel before a creature He has made? Can the Messiah kneel before His subjects? Can the Master kneel before the disciples? Can the Teacher kneel before the student? This is something the world knows nothing of. This is an inversion of the world order. Jesus said, "I have given you an example that ye should also do as I have done to you."

I want you to notice one thing so that the matter becomes inescapable. Every one of those twelve disciples was present. Not only was John there who had such an understanding of the

Lord Jesus and was nearer to His heart than any of the others, but also Peter who was to deny Him with oaths that very night. And all the others denied Him and fled too. We forget that. We often think Peter was the only one, but it says in the Book that all of them did the same. Peter was only the spokesman, and normally spokesmen always get all the trouble. All of them were there. Perhaps the most surprising thing of all was that Judas was there.

I am not sure that many of us, and I must include myself, would wash all the disciples' feet. I think we would say, "Now so and so is going on with the Lord; I will wash so and so's feet. Oh, God is doing something in so and so, I will wash their feet. I do not mind kneeling for a moment before them because I am so delighted with the way they are going. But so and so—I would not give you two pennies for so and so. They are all wind, noisy gong, and clanging cymbal. The sooner someone comes down and bangs them on the head, the better. The sooner somehow or other they come to an end the better." But Jesus washed all their feet.

Now maybe there is somebody in the company where you are whose feet you cannot wash. You could not do this kind of thing with them because it would be misunderstood. Somehow they would take advantage of you. There is no such thing. I must remind you that Judas Iscariot was there, and Jesus washed the feet of Judas. If our Lord can wash the feet of Judas Iscariot, is there a single believer, a single one within the company of the church, whose feet we cannot wash? It is not that we have become a partaker of that one's sins. Jesus knew exactly what was in Judas' heart. Jesus knew that every one of them would deny Him and flee from Him. He knew it all. He knew what was in them.

He prayed for them. He knew exactly what was going to happen, and He washed their feet.

In the States you do not wash people's feet. In fact, the habit of foot washing has gone out more or less altogether except as a ritual in certain denominations at Easter. But in the old days in the Middle East and especially in Israel, when people walked with sandals, their feet got grimed and dirty, filthy. And the first thing you did when a person came to visit you as a mark of respect and love and hospitality was to send a slave to wash the feet. The master did not do it normally nor the owner of a house, but a slave was there on hand to wash the feet.

You all know that when your feet are hot, you are hot, and when your feet are dirty, you feel dirty. That is why the Lord Jesus said to Peter, "You don't need to be bathed. He that is bathed does not need to be washed again." It is only the feet—what we contract through the world in the day to day life.

Here is a ministry that most of us have overlooked and somehow not faced. Most of us have to go out into the world and have contact with the world. Many of you have jobs in the world; you rub shoulders with the world. Even though you are cleansed by the blood of the Lamb, in the way you have to walk each day, you cannot help contracting the defilement and dirt of the world. It is the job of the believers, one to another, just to wash that away, just to refresh the saints. What a wonderful ministry!

Now I am not trying to be funny but normally when we go into a home, we wash our hands, don't we? When you go into a nice home, the first thing they say is, "Do you want to go to the bathroom? There is a towel there and soap." So off you go into the bathroom to wash your hands. Hands are infinitely nicer things than feet. Normally, hands don't smell. Even when they get sweaty and dirty hands are refined.

I know the Chinese never ever shook hands because they did not like to; they did not feel it was clean. They shook their own hands. But the rest of us always shake one another's hands. Do you know why we shake hands? It came from the Roman days. When a person put out his hand, it was clear that there was nothing in it. It showed that there was no dagger in the right hand. That is actually how hand shaking came about. Among the Jewish people, the Hebrew people, it was kissing. They kissed each other on the cheek as the Latin people do to this day. But it was the Roman way to shake hands, and that has slowly traveled through[out] the whole world.

Now, hands are very refined things. Even when they are sweaty and dirty, they are somehow refined. I don't mind taking your hand and shaking it, but your feet? This brings us immediately to the point. There is nothing more unrefined, more vulgar, more crude, more sweaty, more dirty than feet. Jesus washed their feet. It is inescapable. It is very easy to be finished with one another, to be done with one another, to write one another off. But it was the feet that Jesus said we were to wash; perhaps we would say the crudest, most vulgar part of us. This finds me out and it must find you out because all our problems in fellowship come down to feet. We will accept the head, we will accept the hands, but we cannot accept the feet. Jesus said, "I am your Teacher and Master, yet I have washed your feet. I have left you an example that you should do one to another."

Before we finish, there is also one other thing in John's gospel that I would like to point to because all this is what I call the divine method. It is one thing to lay down your life for friends, one thing to lay it down in principle, it is another thing to take it to the *nth* degree. "Love to the uttermost"—that is first love. If you are going to go part of the way why not go the whole way?

Breaking the Alabaster Cruse

> *"Jesus therefore six days before the passover came to Bethany, where Lazarus was, whom Jesus raised from the dead. So they made him a supper there: and Martha served; but Lazarus was one of them that sat at meat with him. Mary therefore took a pound of ointment of pure nard, very precious, and anointed the feet of Jesus, and wiped his feet with her hair: and the house was filled with the odor of the ointment. But Judas Iscariot, one of his disciples, that should betray him, saith, Why was not this ointment sold for three hundred shillings, and given to the poor? Now this he said, not because he cared for the poor; but because he was a thief, and having the bag took away what was put therein. Jesus therefore said, Suffer her to keep it against the day of my burying. For the poor ye have always with you; but me ye have not always." John 12:1–8*

This same story is told again in Matthew 26 and Mark 14, and I think again it reveals the divine method. Not one of those twelve apostles who had been with Jesus for three years and a bit understood what He was facing. Indeed, every time the Lord Jesus spoke about the cross, they said, "Don't talk to us about it. It is not becoming; it is not right. It is darkness in You to think of such a thing. Don't speak about it." But this dear sister with the perception of love, somehow, by the Spirit of God, dimly perceived, dimly understood that Jesus was to die. How great was the extent of her knowledge, I don't know. But her perception led her to identification. She took the most costly thing she had in her home.

In those days, (not today) it was the common thing among Jewish people to keep their savings, because of inflation, in some precious commodity. Many would keep it in spikenard or one of the other precious spices because they were really worth their weight in gold. In other words, they would turn their money into spices or something like that and keep it. There was an added value to turning your savings into spikenard. The burial ritual of the Jewish people was a very costly ritual and required a lot of spikenard. Therefore people often used to keep their savings in spikenard so that if they died or a member of the family died, the spikenard was there to be used for their burial. Maybe it brings it home to you if I tell you that this precious alabaster pot or cruse of spikenard was, in fact, worth one year's wages.

Lazarus and Martha and Mary were not wealthy people. They were not necessarily the poorest of the poor but they were not wealthy people. And this represented something. By the Spirit of God there was the love of God in Mary's heart, there was a sensitivity born of true devotion and love within her, and she perceived that Jesus was going to die. She sensed His loneliness, sensed the fact that maybe no one understood, no one was with Him, no one was touching Him. She must have perhaps prayed and reflected: "Is there anything I could do to stand with Him, to be with Him?" And she suddenly thought, "The alabaster cruse." She took it and broke it, and she poured it over Him. Judas and the disciples were horrified. "A year's wages," Judas said in pompous piety. "We could have fed the poor."

When there is love, it will bring you to be identified with your Lord. This is the divine method. Whithersoever the Lamb goes, you will go. Wherever He leads, you will follow. If it is a valley of the shadow of death, you will go through. If it is into a place of green pastures and still waters, you will follow. If it is into the warfare, you will go. Wherever it is, you follow Him. Into death, into resurrection, you follow Him.

Maybe there is something very precious in your life. Normally there is something that is the most precious thing in our life and until we let it go, we are blocked. I do not know what the alabaster cruse is in your life. I know what it was in mine. But I think every single person intuitively, even if they have never put it into words, knows the alabaster cruse of precious spikenard that is hidden somewhere in their being. That is the thing that the Lord requires you to take. He will not push you. He will not cajole you. He will not pressure you. He will not even say anything. He will leave you. *You* know. You have to take that thing and break it. He will not break it. He will not pour it over Himself. You must pour it over Him.

The Fragrance of Christ

Two things came out of that. The fragrance filled the house. If I know anything about homes in the Middle East, I reckon it filled the houses next door as well. The very street outside would have been permeated with the fragrance of that ointment. Oh, I wish there were more fragrance of the Lord Jesus in my life.

Sadly, so often, it is trapped in an unbroken alabaster cruse. I wish there were more fragrance in our meetings, in our assemblies, in our fellowships. Sadly, it is in unbroken alabaster cruses. We have trapped it inside. The Lord will never thunder at us: "Break it." He leaves us to the work of love. If there is love in us it will identify us so with our Master that in the end, even if it is only on our deathbed, we will take that alabaster cruse and finally break it and pour it all over the Lord. But why wait until a deathbed? Why not do it now?

The Testimony of a Life Filled with Love

Jesus said in Matthew and Mark: "This that she has done shall be told for a memorial to her forever, wherever the gospel is preached." What did He mean? I think He meant that wherever the gospel of the saving love of God is told, the manifestation of it in a life such as Mary's will also be told. It is very easy for us, with our understanding of church truth and of doctrine, of the purpose of God, of the end of God, and the goal of God, to sometimes think that we love the Lord. Then suddenly we come face to face with a person in a community that many of us would write off, and we meet an alabaster cruse that has been broken and poured out. Such in my estimation, and I hope I don't cause any confusion by saying this, is Mother Teresa of Calcutta. Many people could never believe that an abbess in a Roman Catholic convent could be a lover of the Lord Jesus. But that kind of person, more than anybody else, rebukes those of us who have understood the purpose of God and church truth. I do not believe it is just religion. I only wish I had the same devotion and the same sacrifice; that I could only by the grace of God take any alabaster cruse in my life and break it and pour the whole upon Him. In the final analysis, it is our love for Him that is going to determine our love for everyone else.

May God help us, and may we be among that number, that company, who are a manifestation of the love of God. Wherever the gospel is preached, may there be in our lives, in the companies of which we are part, the love of God demonstrated in action. This is the divine method.

We have talked about the divine command, the divine challenge, the divine diagnosis, the divine demonstration, and now the divine method. God has no other way and no other method. The Holy Spirit will touch no other way and no other method. If we would see the house of God built up and completed, if we would see the bride making herself ready for the Bridegroom, if we would come to the throne of God, if we by the grace of God should overcome, it will be by the love of God. May the love wherewith the Father loved the Son be in you and in me, and may Jesus be in you and in me.

Shall we pray?

Oh Lord, only You know where there is an unbroken alabaster cruse of precious ointment. Help us, Lord, we pray by Thy grace, as our love for Thee is kindled to take that precious thing, whatever it is, and break it at Thy feet. Oh Lord, help us in this matter we pray. It is no easy thing for us to go this way, but Lord, we believe that if Thou should kindle our love afresh and cause that love to be shed abroad in our hearts and cause that love to abound yet more and more to the day of Jesus Christ, then somehow we should be enabled to fall into the ground and die, and so shall come a harvest for Thee. So Lord, we shall be enabled to wash one another's feet, even those who are failing the most among us. We shall be enabled dear Lord, by Thy grace to take that—whatever it is—most precious to us, representing as it were our life's work and break it for Thee. Help us Lord, we pray that that love may be in us and Thou in us. We ask it in the name of our Lord Jesus. Amen.

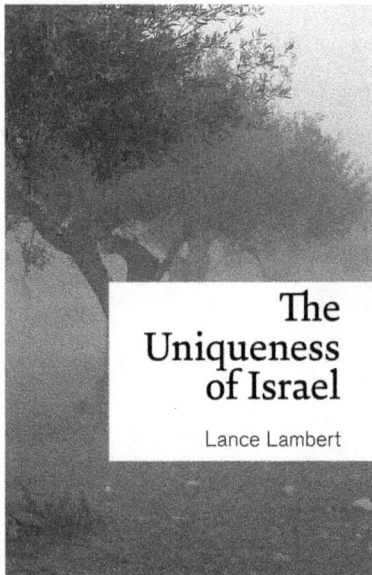

The Uniqueness of Israel

Woven into the fabric of Jewish existence there is an undeniable uniqueness. There is bitter controversy over the subject of Israel, but time itself will establish the truth about this nation's place in God's plan. For Lance Lambert, the Lord Jesus is the key that unlocks Jewish history He is the key not only to their fall, but also to their restoration. For in spite of the fact that they rejected Him, He has not rejected them.

Till The
Day Dawns

Lance Lambert

Till the Day Dawns

"And we have the word of prophecy made more sure; whereunto ye do well that ye take heed, as unto a lamp shining in a dark place, until the day dawn, and the day-star arise in your hearts." (II Peter 1:9).

The word of prophecy was not given that we might merely be comforted but that we would be prepared and made ready. Let us look into the Word of God together, searching out the prophecies, that the Day-Star arise in our hearts until the Day dawns.

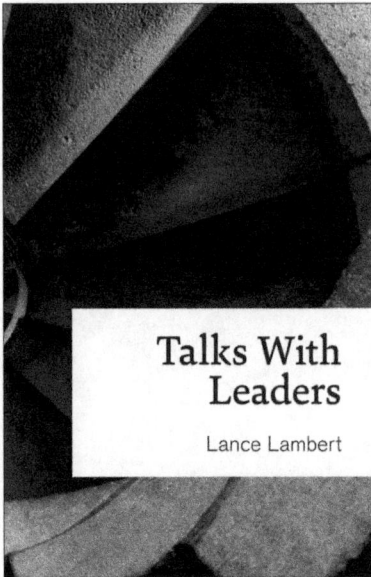

Talks With Leaders

"O Timothy, guard that which is committed unto thee ..." (I Timothy 6:20) Has God given you something? Has God deposited something in you? Is there something of Himself which He has given to you to contribute to the people of God? Guard it. Guard that vision which He has given you. Guard that understanding that He has so mercifully granted to you. Guard that experience which He has given that it does not evaporate or drain away or become a cause of pride. Guard that which the Lord has given to you by the Holy Spirit. In these heart-to-heart talks with leaders Lance Lambert covers such topics as the character of God's servants, the way to serve, the importance of anointing, and hearing God's voice. Let us consider together how to remain faithful with what has been entrusted to us.

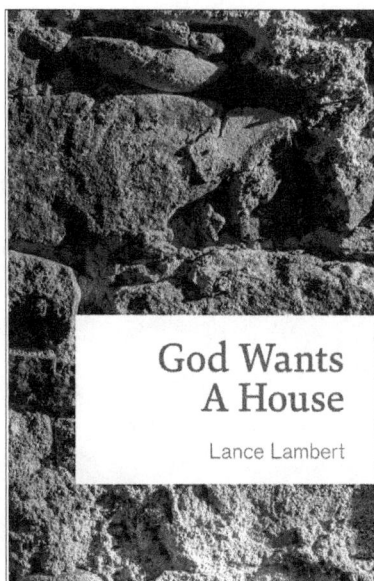

God Wants
A House

Lance Lambert

God Wants a House

Where is God at home? Is He at home in Richmond, VA? Is He at home in Washington? Is He at home in Richmond, Surrey? Is He at home in these other places? Where is God at home? There are thousands of living stones, many, many dear believers with real experience of the Lord, but where has the ark come home? Where are the staves being lengthened that God has finally come home? In God Wants a House Lance looks into this desire of the Lord, this desire He has to dwell with His people. What would this dwelling look like? Let's seek the Lord, that we can say with David, "One thing have I asked of Jehovah, that will I seek after: that I may dwell in the house of Jehovah all the days of my life, To behold the beauty of Jehovah, And to inquire in his temple."